TRAPPED IN SOUND

My Life With Misophonia

Tammy Lee

Platypus Publishing

PLATYPUS
PUBLISHING

Book: Trapped In Sound

For privacy reasons, some names, locations, and dates may have been changed.

Cover and illustrations by Tammy Lee
1st edition 2023

Edited by Tammy Lee

Published by Platypus Publishing

ISBN: 978-1-959555-52-0

For permission requests, contact Tammy Lee.
Email: tammy@gofitlife.ca
Website: https://gofitlife.ca
Mail: PO Box 6282, Fort McMurray, AB, T9H 5N3 Canada

To my beloved parents, Nancy and Vincent, whose unwavering support and encouragement helped me find my strength to keep pushing through.

To my son, Tyler, whose light sparked the transformation within me.

To my soulmate, Justin, whose unconditional acceptance has shown me the true meaning of love.

To my brother, Mark, who always stood up for me through thick and thin.

And to anyone struggling with misophonia.
I hear you, I see you, and I believe you.

CONTENTS

STOP! PLEASE READ

TRIGGER WARNING: This book discusses sounds that may trigger negative emotions for anyone with misophonia. This book also contains language that some people may find offensive. Proceed with caution.

DISCLAIMER: I am not a medical expert or an expert on misophonia. This book and the content provided herein are simply for entertainment purposes and do not take the place of medical advice from your doctor. I do not intend this book to replace therapy or to be taken as any treatment for misophonia. There is nothing scientific contained in this book. It's my personal story. If you decide to try any of my coping mechanisms discussed in this book, you do so at your own risk. Not all coping mechanisms work for everyone. Every person with misophonia experiences it differently. No liability is assumed for losses or damages due to the information provided. You are responsible for your own choices, actions and results. You should first consult with your doctor any mechanism or treatment you wish to pursue.

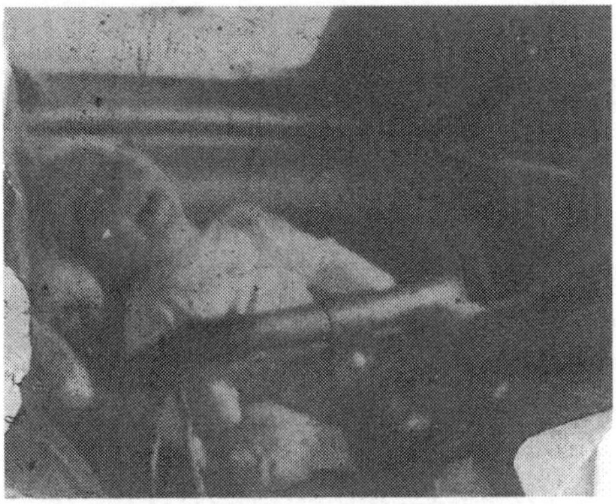

INTRODUCTION

"Mom, tell Mark to stop breathing."

"Mark, stop breathing."

Mark is my younger brother. We were just little kids. This is not even my memory. This is my mother's memory of a time when she was driving down the road with the two of us sitting in the back seat.

Many decades later, when I told my mother I had misophonia, she recalled this memory. Although I don't remember this specific moment in the car's back seat, I certainly remember times during my childhood when I would hit my brother for making breathing sounds.

"Now it all makes sense," she said. "I thought you were just being a hateful snip."

It was the 1970s. Misophonia had yet to be discovered. No one had a clue about what was going on inside my head. So naturally, my outbursts were thought as hateful snips.

Certain sounds cause an extreme emotional response. I will become fixated on it instantly. It's all I can hear, even if you are talking right next to me. I will have difficulty hearing your words because those sounds take over my mind and body.

Rage, anger, hate, disgust... these feelings build. Panic sets in. Whatever I am doing at that moment no longer gets my attention. The only thing I can focus on is that sound. I MUST get it out of my head. If it doesn't stop, I become fearful of how I will behave.

Growing up, I lived like this. I am still living like this. At 50 years old, I have noticed it has worsened as I age.

For many years, I thought I was alone and weird. I have experienced sound rage thousands of times unknowingly having misophonia, and thousands more after discovering it was a thing.

Imagine being a child or an adult and having an extreme emotional reaction to a typical everyday sound in less than a second. I would snap, and no one understood why, not even myself.

Then, at one particular moment, my life changed.

I was attending Acadia University to become a schoolteacher. I learned about misophonia for the very first time while taking an inclusive education course.

That day, I discovered...

I am not a hateful person.
There is a reason for my rage.
This is a real thing.
I am not alone.

Finally, I could begin my journey of understanding and discovery. I could not wait to get home to tell my mother about this.

But, then this happened...

As I started to speak up about what I had discovered, I began to feel more ashamed than ever before. I started to regret my discovery. Was I better off not knowing that I have misophonia? Was I better off keeping it a secret and living a life of silent suffering?

When I tried to explain my condition, I felt no one believed me. People rolled their eyes or told me to "just deal with it." Some made snarky comments like, "Oh yea, that annoys me too, but I just block it out." NO. That's different from how this thing works! I'm not just annoyed. I can't just block it out.

I felt. So. Shut. Down.

But, here's the thing about me. I'm a fighter.

I cannot lie down and let the world run over me. I've survived other traumas in my life. Why would I give up here when I hadn't given up on any other aspect of my life?

And so began the journey to healing from the past, finding my peace, and learning how to protect it. I also had to learn to speak about my misophonia without feeling ashamed.

At the same time, I needed to learn a better way to talk about my misophonia without making others feel like they were to blame for my pain and suffering. Maybe this was where I went wrong before.

I was carrying around so much hurt and anger when I started to talk about it. I felt validated for my behaviour because I had a disorder. This came across as blaming others for it all.

The truth is, they aren't responsible for any of it. No one is responsible for this disorder. It just is, but I am the one who needs to learn how to live with it.

So here I was, not only being solely challenged by sounds but also facing the additional burden of having to change. If I ever wanted to be heard, understood, and supported, I had to find a better way to behave and communicate effectively about my misophonia.

The challenge of living with misophonia will never end. There will always be uncomfortable situations that arise. And accepting that reality is the ultimate conquest.

The world is not going to change for me. I am the one who has to change…for myself.

It will never be perfect, and that's not my expectation. Still, I must dedicate my life to intentional practice to find better ways to live with misophonia.

"You should write a book about that," Justin said. "Call it Choking Hazard."

I giggled.

Justin is my life partner, my soulmate. He heard me say a gazillion times, "I just wanna choke that person right now." He would always respond, "You need to find more effective ways to deal with that because what you're doing isn't helping you."

He was right.

I thought about writing a book and then thought about it some more. Ten years later, after much thought, I finally wrote that book.

Within these pages, I tell you my story in the most vulnerable and honest way possible. You will learn how I lived with misophonia without knowing I had this disorder. I share what happened during the discovery and then how my life changed after that day, and now knowing that I have misophonia.

In search of a greater understanding and awareness, I share how I developed coping mechanisms and better communication methods.

Most importantly, I also discuss my current focus to learn how to manage my misophonia and minimize its control over my life.

I hope that others living with misophonia find someone they can relate to within these pages. Hopefully, they will become inspired to create peace and build the confidence to speak up.

I also hope those who do not have misophonia can gain a deeper understanding to provide better support and genuine compassion for those with this disorder. There is a vast misunderstanding of misophonia in the education system, the workplace, and at home.

Since I started telling others about my story and speaking on social media, many people said, "I have never heard of this before. I didn't even know it existed." I have also encountered many doctors, therapists, teachers, and parents who had never heard of misophonia.

Therefore, I want this book to get into everybody's hands because so many people do not even know this is a real disorder.

Because it's not well-known, many people are likely suffering in silence and being held back in some areas of their life. I know what that feels like, which I will explain in my story.

It makes my heart sad. I want to help others find happiness and hope for a better way to live with misophonia.

Finally, I would be lying if I didn't say that I'm also writing this book for myself. I want to continue to learn about my struggles, heal, and push myself never to give up.

I feel a strong urge to tell my story more than ever before, and this book is one of the essential pieces of work I have ever created.

I am here to tell my truth and my experiences, and I hope that it helps others and creates more awareness worldwide.

That is all.
That is a lot.

So now that you understand my intention, let’s begin.

CHAPTER 1: WHAT IS MISOPHONIA?

"Oh, that sound bothers me too, but I just block it out."

Umm, that's not misophonia. That's an annoyance. There's a difference.

What I have is a disorder. You cannot control it on a conscious level with deliberate intention. You can't just block it out.

My Lord, I only wish it was that simple. All my issues would be solved. There would be no need to write this book.

Misophonia is a selective sound sensitivity disorder that causes an extreme emotional reaction to certain sounds. It's extreme because it is an uncontrollable negative emotion toward a particular sound people without misophonia would find completely normal and may not even notice. It causes a fight, flight, or freeze response in the body.

"Miso" means dislike or hatred, and "phonia" means sounds. Therefore, misophonia means "a dislike or hatred of sounds."

For me, dislike is an understatement. It's pure hatred!

I remember this one time while substitute teaching at a junior high school. While walking across the gym floor with one of the school counsellors, I brought up misophonia and asked if she knew about it.

“What is it called again?” she asked.

“Misophonia. It means hatred of sound.”

Instead of asking more about the condition and how it makes me feel, her immediate response was this:

"That is a terrible definition, and you shouldn't be saying it because it makes it sound like a negative thing."

Inside my body, I felt a shot of "Fuck you." Of course, I said nothing back. I didn't even bother continuing the conversation, as I felt frustrated with her response.

Hate is a natural emotion, not a positive one, and it is the intense emotion I feel when triggered.

I get what she was trying to say. A disorder shouldn't come with a negative label, as that can cause other problems. Still, her response assumed I didn't already know that and instead of inquiring more to understand me, she pounced.

This is another example of what I struggle with when discussing this disorder. I sometimes don't even get a chance to go beyond the definition because they have taken over the direction of the conversation.

But in this book, I am in complete control. ***smirky smile****

With "hatred of sounds" only being one definition, I agree that sound sensitivity disorder is a better definition. I use them both because one gives more profound insight into my emotions, and the other describes it as a medical disorder.

So, now you may wonder which sounds trigger me. Not all sounds. They are specific sounds.

Also, a sound that impacts me may not affect another person with the same disorder. We may share some common triggers, but every person with misophonia will still experience it uniquely. Therefore, we cannot all be painted with the same brush.

Unfortunately, over the last two decades, I have noticed that my triggers are expanding into visuals. This is called misokensia, aka "hatred of movements."

I no longer have to hear someone chewing gum to be triggered. All I need is to see someone chewing it, and the emotions are instantly evoked – starting with disgust. The feelings become amplified if I continue to see and hear them together. Rage and disgust boil up inside.

I try as hard as possible not to look at the person because it heightens my state. Sometimes this isn't easy to do if they try to converse with me.

Think about that for a moment, even if you don't have misophonia. Just try to imagine that situation...

Even the written word of a trigger can cause a reaction because it can be associated with a sound memory. It is common to see "Trigger Warning" included in a post within misophonia support groups on Facebook. That is why I added a trigger warning at the beginning of this book.

Reading about sound triggers doesn't impact me the same way as hearing them, but recalling memories can make me emotional. There have been some hard days in writing this book. I wish I could erase some memories from my mind for good.

Honestly, I can see why some people have difficulty understanding me or think it's a psychological issue. However, it is not.

Misophonia is a brain-based neurophysiological disorder that needs more research to understand better.

"Only officially recognized as a medical disorder in 2001, misophonia is a condition characterized by severe sensitivity to certain sounds." It was coined by neurophysiologist Pawel Jastreboff, who wrote a paper describing symptoms of decreased sound tolerance in 2001. (1)

While this book is about my story, the science of misophonia is also essential. Therefore, at the end of this book, I include a short list of additional resources to learn more.

I'm not an expert on misophonia, and while you won't learn the 'sciency' stuff from me, you will undoubtedly learn how it can impact one's life.

The next chapter will provide more insight into this disorder and what happens inside my body and mind when I hear a sound that triggers me.

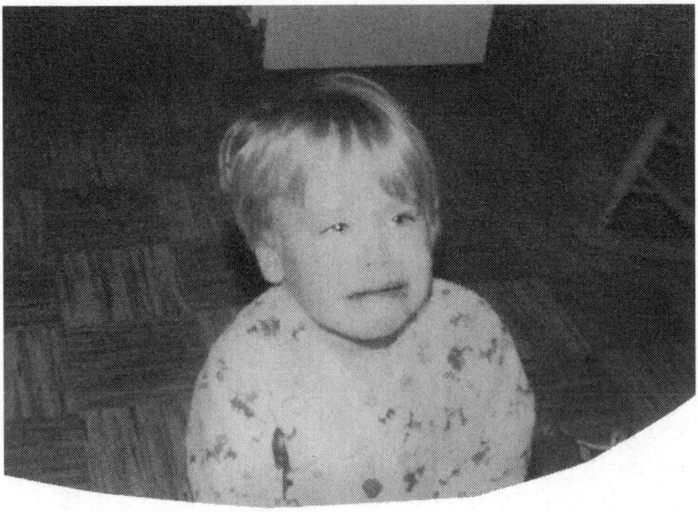

CHAPTER 2: HOW IT MAKES ME FEEL

Inside my head: "Snap that gum one more time, and I will annihilate you."

No, I would not, but these aggressive and violent thoughts come into my head when I hear someone popping gum. And I can't help it. It's an automatic feeling.

Let's first begin by listing my primary triggers. This list is not static. Instead, it's dynamic. The severity of the emotional reaction is getting more intense as I age, and the list is growing.

I don't recall having many triggers when I was a child, not like I do now. Through my teen years, I can remember additional new triggers, especially after I started having my period. Regular exposure to sounds that trigger me has also heightened my emotional response.

My sound trigger list below is challenging to write. I cringe as I type it out.

- Barking dog and other animal sounds, such as licking fur or chewing a bone.
- Nasal sounds, such as heavy breathing or whistling noise from a dry nose.
- Mouth sounds such as breathing, clearing the throat, smacking lips, eating, chewing, slurping, crunching, and so on.
- Talking with food in the mouth, especially if it is halfway down the throat.
- Smacking lips or tongue off the roof of your mouth in between words during a discussion.
- Gum chewing, blowing bubbles, snapping and cracking it, cough drops or hard candy rattling around in one's mouth, or sucking on them.
- Picking teeth, biting nails, clipping nails, any sounds with teeth and nails.
- Whistling through lips or teeth, humming, unnecessary but intentional mouth noises that people make to entertain themselves.
- High-pitched frequencies, smoke alarms, beeps in a grocery store, etc.
- Rumbling bass in which sounds are muffled, like through a floor, wall, or mattress (i.e., snoring).

- Vibrations; it's like I can hear the trigger sound through the feel of it.
- Repeated sounds (tap dripping, pen clicking, foot or finger tapping, ticking clock).
- Some music - depends on the beat, tone, or if I hear a repetitive loop.
- Certain voices (i.e., froggy voice) and the way some people pronounce words (sharp 's' and 't').
- Kitchen sounds such as dishes and utensils clanging (i.e., restaurants with open kitchens where all the echoing sounds fill my head with misery).
- Loud sudden bangs, loud echoes.
- Scratchy or screechy noises from technology, such as someone talking on a speaker or a radio that isn't fully tuned (this is a growing problem with how people use iPhones and iPads in public, like at a restaurant, or with phone calls, music or kids' games on speaker).
- Persistent noises that continue to happen over time, causing a slow build-up of rage, such as a tick in a vehicle while driving or a squeak coming from my bicycle.

There's more, but this is enough to show you that the various triggers are broad. They are not just from humans but also animals, things, and within specific spaces.

Now that you have my main list, I'll explain what happens inside me when I hear these sounds.

Sometimes, I explain it like this…

If you were walking in the woods and suddenly saw a bear, you may instantly feel panic and fear. You may want to run away, or you can't move. Confusion sets in.

Now, add rage and disgust to that, and allow it to rise higher and higher as you stand there. So much is happening inside your head. Many feelings are rushing through your body, your heart is pounding, and you begin to sweat.

These are the emotions I feel. The longer I am subjected to the sound, the more the feelings pile up. Sometimes it's an instant explosion, and sometimes it builds in layers.

It can happen in less than a millisecond. For example, a dog's first bark doesn't even have to be completed, and I'm already enraged. The more it barks, the hotter my blood boils.

I feel it in my chest and my head. My heart pumps harder, and my breathing becomes rapid. Whatever thoughts were in my mind were now gone. The sound now consumes the entire brain space.

I become fixated on it, and can lose track of where I am in space. Sometimes I may bump into someone or something and become frantic. The sound needs to stop. I need to escape.

My voice changes. As my body fills with anger, my facial expressions change. I feel like I just stepped into a world of chaos.

I can go from sitting calmly in a chair to quickly getting up out of the chair with panic. My movements become quick and snappy. I'm seeking the source of the sound.

Maybe I can stop it if I can find it. I need to escape if I can't stop it. The meltdown begins if I can't escape.

I feel like I am losing control. I have to help myself get through it. It's like I am splitting into two people. One person struggles to remain in control while the other is in a fight. It's hard to hide.

If it persists, I feel adrenaline rushing, anxiety skyrocketing, heart pounding harder. Panic and fear set in. I'm going fucking mad. I can't stop the sound. I have no control.

But rage isn't the only thing I feel. Hate and disgust are big emotions I also feel. I can hate someone I love. I don't actually hate that person, but I hate them at that moment.

The hate I feel isn't like hating someone because I don't like them. It's not a permanent thing. It's temporary. I hate the sounds they make, and so it is an association. It creates this thing I call a “hate glitch".

Same with disgust. The person is not disgusting in general, but the sound creates a feeling of disgust. In my head, I'm thinking, "that's fucking disgusting." And again, it's like a glitch.

Telling someone I hate them and that they are disgusting is not something I want to say to anyone. Still, I feel these feelings when they make the trigger sounds. When they stop making the sound, the feelings go away.

Yes, I have told people I hated them and thought they were disgusting. I didn't know what was wrong with me. I blamed them.

I always felt that they could stop the sound if they wanted to...if only they would eat with their mouth closed, spit out their gum, and stop whistling.

And as much as I hate to admit this, I also thought, "if you got healthy, you wouldn't have to breathe like that."

But these feelings and thoughts are not a reflection of my true self. To release my frustration, I would take it out on them, blaming them at every level possible. I don't feel that way, but I sure do in the heat of the moment.

See what I mean? It is challenging to explain. I don't want to admit any of this. The person on the receiving end isn't going to understand because it makes no sense. It sounds irrational, and it also sounds downright mean and ignorant.

These feelings make it extremely challenging to establish good relationships. I can't talk about how someone is triggering me because I don't want to make them feel bad, so it seems like I am an asshole because of how I behave.

To make matters worse, if I feel trapped to the point of explosion, I start screaming and yelling. I have become violent and out of control. The "fight" response has been ignited. I have hit people. I have even hit myself.

In situations where I have been able to escape, I crumble and cry. I have to pull myself together with deep breathing, self-talk, and maybe even express some pent-up anger by punching something. Exercise has helped me immensely, which I will talk about later.

You might think what a relief it must be for me when the sound ends. Nope, it doesn't end. It is not over. I can still hear it in my head. Maybe even for another 5 – 10 minutes, or even off and on throughout the rest of the day.

Even a decade later, I can still hear the sound in traumatic situations. When I recall the memory associated with a severe trigger, I can feel a physiological response. My heart pounds, my breathing becomes shallow, and a shiver goes up my spine...I feel rage, hate and disgust. It usually makes me cry.

A specific sound is embedded in my memory. This acts as a preventative measure and has trained me to be wary of particular places, people, and situations because I NEVER want to be around a sound like that ever again. That is the "PTSD" part of my misophonia.

Finally, the last thing I need to explain is a biggie. This one gets people.

“Why can you make the sounds you hate and not feel triggered.”

The simple answer – I am in control! At any point, I can make the sound stop.

I can chew gum, click pens, smack my lips, crunch chips, and breathe heavily, but no, you cannot!

Trying to tell people this has never been a success. They think I'm a hypocrite and making shit up.

Explaining the different aspects and feelings of misophonia has always been challenging, even with people who seemed to be listening and supportive. When a situation arises, though, that's when true colours shine.

My friend and I were on a road trip. I heard a noise in the vehicle. She knew about my misophonia, so I felt comfortable telling her about a sound triggering me. I asked her to try and find it so we could stop it.

She searched around but couldn't locate the sound's origin. I could feel the emotions building as the sound continued. I was pushing her to find the sound, but I was not yelling or being rude. I just needed the sound to stop and wanted her to try harder.

My left ear has "super-sonic" hearing. If I listen to the sound with intention, I can dial in the type of sound and location. I identified the sound as keys, and it seemed like they were coming from her purse.

I asked her to check. For some reason, she was resistant and ignored my request by looking in other spots. Maybe she felt that I was blaming her?

Several more times, I asked, "Please look in your purse. It sounds like keys." Finally, she did. I was right. It was her keys.

But here's the sucky part about this whole situation...

That incident created an extremely uncomfortable and awkward feeling between us. I noticed a change in my friend's body language, face, and attitude. She was annoyed, and now I had to deal with her attitude toward me.

This is why I am writing my story. I want people to stop making those of us with misophonia feel like we are annoying freaks.

I often get blamed for causing inconvenient situations over a typical noise that those who do not have misophonia can easily block out.

The struggle is real. I know the noise isn't a threat, but I can't stop my brain from interpreting it that way.

I lose myself if multiple trigger sounds happen at once or if I'm overstimulated by too much noise. I have fled grocery stores, walked out of waiting rooms, left family gatherings, and so on.

My mind snaps, and I have to get out quickly. I sit in my car after escaping and cry. I am feeling like a freak. I have curled myself up on the basement floor of my house with earplugs, praying to God to make it stop.

People do not realize how debilitating this can be. People need to learn how misophonia works.

Telling my story is hard because it requires admitting things that I have never spoken about before, exposing myself in the most vulnerable way. And I fear hurting the people I love.

But if I can't tell my story honestly, there is no sense in telling it. And I hope this book does what I want it to do – create a greater understanding.

Now that I have set the stage by explaining misophonia, sharing my biggest triggers and how it makes me feel, I can tell my story.

Here we go.

CHAPTER 3: TRAPPED IN SOUND

The emotions build, becoming more potent by the second, and I have no place to go. I can't escape. I can't stop the sounds. I have to endure it, and I have no idea when it will end.

I am trapped by sound.

Home, school, church, family gatherings, waiting rooms, grocery stores, shopping centres, restaurants, line-ups, funerals, movie theatres, neighbourhoods...

All these people are making noises. They fill all these spaces with sounds.

The fear of being trapped by sounds that trigger me is an ongoing concern in my everyday life.

I am learning ways to cope, but that doesn't mean I can't feel trapped. I am getting better at identifying where the traps are located and how to escape them if I become trapped. Sometimes that is impossible.

Let me explain...

Suppose I am forced to sit next to someone making sounds that trigger me. I can't leave. I feel trapped. When I feel trapped, it amplifies the entire experience.

As I fill with rage, I also feel panic. My body draws inward like I want to turn myself inside out. If there were something I could evolve into, it would be the devil.

Pretty sure that person sitting next to me thinks I'm a snot. My body language isn't exactly welcoming. I want to connect, but I fear starting a discussion because what if I am triggered by the sound of their voice or how they pronounce certain letters or words? I would become frustrated and then ask, "Why did I just do that to myself?"

Questions circle inside my head. What if they repeatedly say 'Umm,' smack the roof of their mouth with their tongue, and make sharp 's' and 't' sounds?

I won't be able to focus on what they say anyway because all I will hear are these sounds and the feeling that I will burst into a ball of flames and choke them.

This is my misophonia version of “Stranger Danger”. Any place I am required to sit next to a stranger creates great anxiety. Waiting rooms, movie theatres, line-ups, classrooms, funerals, weddings, churches, etc. The thought of possibly sitting next to someone who triggers me and not being able to escape is a constant worry.

Every day is like this: "Will there be a sound, and how will I be able to handle it today?" Sometimes, I stay home, especially when I'm already an emotional mess for other reasons unrelated to misophonia.

Airplanes are one of the worst places for me to be and have the highest number of sound traps. Not only are planes noisy, but the people on them are too. When I have to fly, I prepare mentally and emotionally for weeks ahead.

Sitting next to someone who snores is an absolute nightmare. It is pure hell. I can't escape it. Unfortunately, earplugs don't block out that sound, and I can feel the vibrations.

People may bring their dogs on the plane. The dog whines and cries and lets out frequent yelps. This makes my brain feel like it is being stabbed with a fork each time. It causes physical and emotional pain for the entire trip.

By the time I get off the plane, I'm a wreck. I need to release it. I walk around to empty my head of the horrible experience and wear off the emotions.

Sometimes I book a seat in business class when I fly. If I were rich, I would reserve all the seats next to me, in front of me and behind me so that I could have all the space without people in it—a pipe dream.

Classrooms have also been a sound trap all my life. I would have to become fixated on something to help me get through class. My teachers often accused me of daydreaming.

I would fidget in my seat and move around a lot, trying to find a way to distract my mind from the noise and release some of the pent-up frustration.

As the emotions would roll around in my body, I would get more fidgety. I was uncomfortable, but my teachers never saw it like that. They saw it as disruptive, rude, ignorant, or obnoxious.

I'm not blaming them. They didn't know. No one did. I was in school from 1977 to 1990. The term misophonia was not coined until 2001.

Sometimes, when I am trapped and able to identify the sound makers, I feel the compulsive urge to stare at them, hoping that somehow it will make them stop.

But the reality is that they have no idea they are making a noise that is driving me insane. If I stare too much, they eventually notice. They detect the hate. I don't hate them, but I hate the sound they make. I want so badly for them to stop, and I struggle to stop staring at them.

Sometimes I am asked, “Is there something wrong?”

How do I say, "Yeah, you're fuckin' making a sound that's driving me nuts. Stop it!"

I certainly don't say this. I may bring it up if I know the person well and feel comfortable opening up. Also, I need to feel mentally strong enough to say it kindly while keeping my internal rage in check.

I have been blunt with loved ones and hurt them. When I felt trapped by a sound and couldn't get away, the rage was building, and I had lost control.

I have opened my mouth to try and explain, but what came out is not what I ever wanted to hear myself say. It caused a situation. I had to apologize, and I couldn't erase the hurt. Now I had to deal with that on top of everything else.

Feeling trapped for an extended period around a high-trigger sound has caused me so much trauma. When I recall specific memories, my heart pounds the same, I hear the same sound in my head, the rage builds, and the emotions rush in.

These still make me cry, become extremely angry, or fill me with so much disgust that I can lose my appetite, even after a decade or more has passed. These extreme situations have scarred me permanently.

Almost ten years ago, we lost a very close family friend. A celebration of his life was held in another friend's home. I will refer to this person as the "host".

I was in the kitchen mulling over the food when the host came in. Instantly, I noticed his breathing, very nasally, loud, non-stop, in and out, in and out... a sound at the top of my severe trigger list.

And as soon as he started to eat, my emotions doubled. Disgusting! It's all I could hear over everything else. Over the chatter and music, it filled my head, and I started to panic.

I am at a dear friend's celebration of life. I just arrived and have only been there for about five minutes, and now I want to leave immediately and as fast as possible.

The wife of the friend who passed away came up to me and thanked me for coming, gave me a big warm hug, and we had a small chat.

The host stood by us, listening and eating. I had difficulty focusing on the lady speaking to me, who deserved my full attention, compassion, and love.

Inside my body, I was cringing, full of hate and disgust, feelings getting stronger with every second passing while he made those sounds.

I kept telling myself, "Stay calm, Tammy. Keep it together."

Then, this happened...

"Have you ever been in this house before?" she asked.

"No," I answered.

She turned to the host and said, "Shall we give her a tour."

"Of course," he said.

He grabbed a napkin and some more food, and I almost fell to the floor. Is this really happening?

Dear Lord, give me the strength to see this through. Please help me to remain calm, polite, and loving. Don't show your emotions, for the love of God, don't show a damn thing.

I just stepped into the worst kind of hell!

So much going on inside me, and no one knows it's happening. My body felt like it was crumbling inward. I could feel my chest collapse. Movements became slow. I had to force myself to follow. I know I can wear the emotions on my face, so I had to battle that too.

I followed them up the stairs, just the three of us. I didn't want to go. It took a lot of mental work to take each step. I wanted to leave so badly. My heart was pounding. I was cringing as the sounds filled my entire being.

As we moved through each room, his breathing and eating got louder. Every time my face was out of sight, I could feel it wrinkle up in disgust. At this point, I'm fighting tears. Don't let them come into my eyes...

I wanted to fucking choke him. I imagined putting my hands over his face and saying, "Stop fuckin' breathing. You are so disgusting!" I did all I could do not to mimic the sounds he was making. I wanted to mock him and demonstrate how gross he was behaving.

And the whole time they gave me this Tour of Hell, I never heard a single word they said. I had to force myself to pay attention and at least respond with something to seem okay. But I was not okay.

When the tour was complete, the wife hugged me. She could sense something was wrong, but we didn't discuss it. After all, it's a celebration of her husband's life. It's normal to seem emotional in situations like this. But she didn't know what was truly wrong, and I wasn't about to tell her.

My mom was sitting in the living room with many other people visiting that day. I sat in a chair, staring at the floor. She looked at me. She knew something was wrong...very, very wrong, but she didn't know what.

I hated to do it, but I got up and left. I couldn't get the noise out of my head, and I couldn't shake the feelings inside me.

They were circling in my body, looking for a way out. There was no escape or way to release the rage, so I had to leave. I wasn't sure how much longer I could control myself.

I went over to my mom and hugged her. I told her I loved her and would talk to her later. She was worried, and I could feel that. I wanted to cry and have her hold me. I felt utterly broken. Just remembering this as I write, my eyes are filled with tears.

I said goodbye to the wife and left. I didn't even say anything to the host. I didn't want to be anywhere near him. I felt so terrible, but I was destroyed.

When I got into my car, I screamed. I pounded the steering wheel. I sat there, tears streaming down my face, trembling from head to toe, trying to get his sounds out of my head.

I couldn't drive like that. I couldn't sit there for much longer, fearing someone would notice and come out to see what was happening. I needed to get my shit together.

I wiped my tears, took a few deep breaths, started the car and drove home. His sounds remained in my head for a long time. The rest of my day was impacted by this extreme emotional situation of feeling trapped without escape. It was intense.

Almost a decade later, I still feel the pain as I write this. If I had a magic wand, I would wipe this entire memory from my mind. I don't want it. I don't want any other memories like this, either.

Eventually, I told my mom what had happened. She felt so sad for me, and she held me for a while.

As hard as it is to tell, this story sends a critical message to my readers. It can be severely traumatizing when you force someone with misophonia to remain in a situation where sounds emotionally trigger them.

I sometimes panic in certain situations, recalling the emotional trauma. Situations like this increase the intensity of a trigger. The emotional reaction becomes quicker and more intense because the memory of the emotional trauma during the initial exposure creates panic and fear of it happening again. I don't want to relive that moment, and I will do whatever I can to avoid it.

But sadly, these events are unpredictable. Being trapped by a sound without escape is the worst-case scenario for me, living with misophonia. Because I know this, I constantly observe, analyze, and collect data on where these traps might be located. However, sometimes I am wrong or fail, and suddenly, I find myself in another sound trap.

Now that I know I have misophonia, I seek escape routes and more effective ways to communicate with people. If an incident arises, I can leave. When I have to go, I need to do so as quickly as possible.

Not too long ago, I was grocery shopping at my usual place. There were so many trigger sounds in the store that day. Having my period exacerbated my sound sensitivity.

The whistling, the gum-snapping, squeaky wheels, the scratchy music over the sound system. It was piling up in my brain. The rage was building. I couldn't even look up. I stared at the floor and froze, although I wanted to take my cart and ram it into the shelves and scream and yell, "Fuck off, just fuck off with all the noise!"

My cart was half-filled. I snapped. I walked away and left the store. I could not take it. I couldn't stay. Not even long enough to put my groceries back on the shelves.

My heart was pounding. I was shaking. I got into my vehicle and sat inside and cried. It took me several minutes to calm down. The usual try to "untraumatize myself" routine.

I drove home with no groceries. I didn't care. There was always another day.

But it's getting harder to get outside. People and places worry me as my misophonia gets worse.

"Are they going to make sounds? Will they fill the space with sounds?"

Every time I walk into a waiting room, stand in line, sit next to someone on an airplane, or meet a new client, I think, "Brace yourself, Tammy. Prepare!"

I wish I could walk around wearing complete noise-cancelling earmuffs and learn how to read lips and do sign language. Maybe I should pretend I'm deaf. I know that sounds terrible and offensive, but this disorder makes me feel like I'm evil.

One of the hardest things about having misophonia is telling the truth about my feelings. They are about hate, rage, and disgust, all incredibly negative emotions. I come off as a mean and ignorant asshole that lacks compassion for others.

The truth is, I'm the complete opposite, but people judge and assume, even when I try to explain.

All my life, I have lived with these labels. It's why I am now trying so hard to be kinder. The older I get, the worse my

misophonia gets, so the need to combat my hate with love is more important than ever.

I know better now too. I must work at it if I want to live a happier life. No one is responsible for this, not even me. This is a disorder, and I have to live with it.

And while I do care about my behaviour and how I come across, it's not easy to control. People need to be more patient with me, and I have to give myself room. One day at a time...

I am well aware of my behaviour.
I am well aware that you do not understand it.
Can we please work together?

I am doing everything in my power to understand this disorder. I work daily to ensure I don't treat others poorly, even though my body and mind are full of sound rage.

And the more I push to understand what I need to gain a sense of control, the more I can identify and escape the sound traps and protect my peace. I need this for my happiness. I want to lay my head down at night and feel good about the person I am and how I treat others. Isn't that what we all want?

This is my life with misophonia. It's not easy. It never will be.

I have accepted that, but I won't be ruled by it.

I will create the rules.

CHAPTER 4: YOU'RE A HATEFUL SNIP

Having misophonia as a child is very different as a teen or adult. I hit my brother when I was little, but I would never hit him now. I would throw tantrums, snip people off, be hard to talk to, and be aggressive. As I grew older, I became more aware of how I was acting, and it has tapered down, for the most part.

Mom and Dad thought I was a snip. They weren't wrong. I was. I got angry, and I acted out.

Although I don't have many childhood memories of my misophonia, I know I had it. It got worse during my teen years with more triggers and heightened responses. I can't remember when it started, but I can't remember not having it either.

Imagine growing up with sounds triggering an emotional reaction and not understanding anything about it. I never talked about the feelings I felt. I didn't get it. I just reacted. Looking at me from the outside, you would think I was a hateful snip.

Suppertime was the worst time of day. We always had supper together at the table. It was a family tradition. I wanted to eat away from the table, but we weren't allowed to eat in the living room or our bedrooms. I had to put up with all the eating noises.

I don't know how old I was, but it was around my mid-teens. We were all eating at the dinner table. My grandmother, who I call Nanny, was there.

Mom and Nanny were both making the most unbelievable eating sounds. I whispered under my breath, "That's disgusting." Those were my exact words. I remember it clearly. I also remember feeling so compelled to say it. I didn't want to say it, but it came out because the tension needed to be released.

I wanted to stand up and tell them how disgusting they were and how much I couldn't stand watching them eat. I wanted to show them how gross they were and imitate the awful sounds they were making. I wanted to mock them by breathing heavily, shoving food in my mouth, and talking with it going down my throat.

Ugh. That is so hard to admit. I never told anyone until now. I love my mom and nanny and never wanted to hurt them emotionally or physically. This disorder just made me feel these things. And I didn't understand.

When I whispered these words, I didn't whisper them quietly enough. My dad heard them but thought I said, "You're disgusting," and he knew I was directing it toward my mother. While he wasn't wrong, he wasn't right either.

Regardless, what happened next was a build-up of my dad's frustration and feeling sick and tired of my attitude. He snapped.

He accused me of calling my mom disgusting. I denied it. He said he heard it, and the argument became heated. Dad stood up from the table, picked me up from my chair, and pushed me out the back door...no shoes on...no jacket.

Instead of trying to get back in the house, I started running down the driveway and onto the road. I remember there was snow on the ground. I didn't care. I wanted to run away. I never wanted to go back to those sounds.

My heart was pounding, tears were streaming down my face, feet were frozen, but I weirdly felt relieved as the sounds were gone. I could now scream and cry and let go of all the frustrations I was holding inside my body at the supper table.

Soon, my brother came up behind me. He was there to save me and comfort me. He piggy-backed me home. We came into the house, and I went straight to my room.

Another day in the life of a snippy teenager unknowingly having misophonia. Brutal. Disturbing. Traumatizing. I was a hateful fucking person.

No, of course, I don't blame my dad. I don't hold anything against him. He couldn't take it anymore. I was a challenging person to live with.

"You need an attitude adjustment." I heard that a lot.

Yes, I did, but no one understood the root cause of it all. I was silent about my emotions towards certain sounds. It was just messy.

I graduated from high school in June of 1990 at age 18. One day the following summer, when my parents were at a local community event, I packed my bags and moved out.

I left a note on the table. I can't remember what I wrote, but it probably wasn't pleasant. I know this tore my mother apart, but there was a sense of relief within the family. I caused a lot of friction in that house, especially as a teenager. I wasn't getting easier to live with as the years went by.

For me, getting away was like escaping a house jam-packed with sound triggers. I moved into a bachelor's apartment and was free of the daily sounds driving me insane.

But, within a year, I moved back in with Mom and Dad. It only lasted two months. I moved out and, again, not on a good note. As much as I wanted to be with my family, I couldn't. It created an internal war between love and rage, blazing hotter as the years passed.

I used to go on about how abused I was growing up. I'm not afraid to admit I was a challenge and caused much stress in our household. I hold nothing against my parents about how they treated me when I acted out. When I finally grew up and learned about my misophonia, I realized I was just as much the abuser.

None of us knew what the hell was going on with me. My parents are not mean people. Everyone who knows my parents knows they would never intentionally cause me pain and suffering.

My dad would give his only shirt off his back to a stranger. My mom has a unique ability to forgive others and move on without losing compassion.

Regardless of how I behaved, they hugged me and told me they loved me throughout my entire life.

It doesn't matter which way you look at it. I had a disorder that made me feel rage, anger, hate, and disgust daily.

Even though I fought hard to hold much of it back and spent a lot of time in my room so I could free my mind, I often expressed these emotions in outbursts and a hateful attitude.

I was angry—a lot. And I feel like this disorder trained me to be like that. Because anger became a daily emotion, I became desensitized to the feeling and normalized it. If triggered, I could flip like a switch. Because I didn't understand it, I just let it go.

Releasing the anger released the built-up tension. It felt good to get it out, like I was emptying a cramped space, suffocating me.

But the aftermath was so destructive and heartbreaking. I was not wholly aware of the problems I was causing because I was so confused about what the hell was going on with me.

Looking back over my life, growing up with my parents, I feel my teen years were some of the most fucked up years of my life.

Who was I? What the hell was wrong with me? It's embarrassing. I'm weird. No one likes me. I'm not that nice. I need to be alone.

I feel terrible heartache for how I treated my parents and brother. So many fights, yelling and screaming. If only I had known. How different things would have been.

Misophonia robbed me of experiences I wish I could have had with my family. Being around them was always an internal battle for me. My room was where I spent much of my time.

This doesn't mean I didn't have good times. I have many beautiful memories. My parents are loving and supportive, but I could have gotten so much more out of it had I not been this way. It divided us. It was me against them. I felt like the proverbial black sheep.

It is hard to admit all of this. I was a hateful snip and hard to live with. I have accepted it because I can't heal otherwise. If I don't face reality, then I can't repair the damage done to my family and myself.

People now tell me not to be so hard on myself. I can't entirely agree. I have to be hard on myself because sometimes that is what it takes to dig deep enough to make a difference.

And the real change started to happen when I finally found out what was wrong with me. That's when I could make sense of all those years and begin to recreate what I had lost with my family.

I thank my lucky stars that my family has been so forgiving. I can't imagine where I would be right now if they had never let me back in, time and time again.

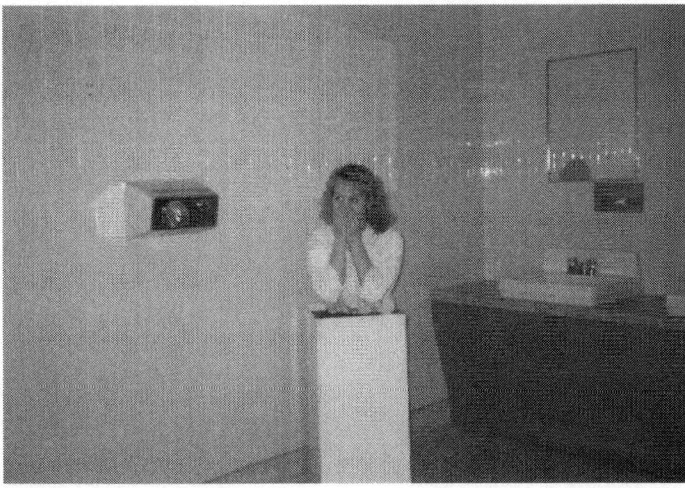

CHAPTER 5: SCHOOL WASN'T COOL

School was not always cool. Not at all.
I wanted to be there but also didn't.
It felt impossible at times.

The classrooms were noisy. I felt awkward and uncomfortable and could not settle in. I was curious about things, but my thoughts were often interrupted, which frustrated me.

The sound of a chair scraping across the floor, a student sitting next to me breathing loudly, sick kids sniffling and coughing, pens clicking, chalk on the board, squeaky sneakers, gym whistle, bouncing balls, school bell, announcements over a scratchy speaker, screaming kids...UGH!

This was my daily hell, from home to school, from school to home.

And the bus ride to and from? Do I really need to explain...

Trying to maintain focus was a constant, arduous struggle. Often, I just threw in the towel. I can't do this. And so, I heard many times over...

"Sit in your seat."
"Pay attention."
"Stop talking."
"Stop daydreaming."
"Your assignment is late."
"You need to participate more."
"You're disrupting the class."
"Get out!"

I didn't pay attention. I was busy doing other stuff in my head, like trying to survive. I couldn't get away. I couldn't cover my ears, which would have been weird, so I had to sit there and listen to it all.

My eyes would dart left to right, searching for some distraction to take my focus away from the noise. Sometimes I would stare at my workbook or the wall, trying to get lost somewhere else in my head.

One time in grade 6, my teacher hit me over the head with a textbook and told me to stop daydreaming. When she hit me, my body was already filled with rage from trying to deal with the student breathing heavily behind me.

I wanted to punch her. My face turned red from embarrassment. I felt so ashamed in front of all my peers, but mostly I felt anger. I hated that teacher.

I didn't have excellent grades in school. I often needed clarification, missed instructions, struggled to pay attention...blah blah blah.

I was withdrawn. Weird. I always felt awkward, and I acted that way too. I didn't fit in anywhere. I had a best friend for a while, but she eventually left me. I had no one, really.

I was bullied throughout my elementary and junior high school years. That just amplified the stuff I was already struggling with. I became bitter and mean and wore that on my sleeve. I had a hard time making friends.

In junior high, we had more freedom to move about. Group work, change up classrooms for different subjects, and I could go outside more often, had a more extensive playground to explore with quieter spaces. I could walk the hallways and find my quiet little places, such as under the stairs or in the corner of an empty classroom. It was good sometimes.

I often talked in class. I could attempt to overpower the sounds, making me feel like I had some control. I was moved around a lot in class and often accused of disrupting.

In grade 7, my teacher moved me nine times. In grade 8, I was sometimes kicked out of the classroom. I had to stand in the hallway or was sent to the office. Getting kicked out was a chance to escape. I felt guilty because I didn't want to upset the teacher, but I was free from the noise.

I was becoming violent at school. I got into physical fights with students, both boys and girls—anyone who picked on me. In elementary, I was too scared to lash out, but I started to let it go in junior high.

I wasn't a stranger to the act of punching someone. I beat on my brother and sometimes my cousins and friends outside of school. I even hit my mother. If I could hit my mother, I could punch anyone.

It didn't take much for me to boil over with a pot of anger, always simmering on the stove. I fought in hallways, classrooms, schoolyards and on the bus.

One time in grade 9, a girl came up to me and accused me of smearing her name on the door of a bathroom stall. She stuck her finger in my face, and spit flew from her mouth as she yelled at me.

I stood there watching her, and I could feel the rage building from the bottom up. I started chopping toward her finger as if I were going to bite it. She kept edging closer, and then I snapped.

I gave her a quick push and then punched her straight in the face with a closed fist. She ran out the door and probably didn't expect me to react that way. It's not typical behaviour.

One day while riding the school bus home, a boy was sitting in front of me. He kept turning around, mocking me and making annoying sounds. Without a word, I jumped up and punched him. We both were moved to the front of the bus for a while.

When I moved to senior high, I didn't get in fights as much. It was a different vibe, and I had more space. I also became more conscious about how I behaved as I grew older.

I joined a peer counselling program to try and better myself. I could learn how to be kinder to others by helping them. While I'm glad I did it for the experience, it didn't stop the angry outbursts.

In senior high, I also had the freedom to pick some subjects, which improved my focus and attention. I could learn exciting things about sociology, photography, and geology. Sometimes I was allowed to move out of my seat freely without worrying about getting into trouble. My mind was preoccupied.

You would think I would have taken up sports as a positive outlet. I didn't have those opportunities or support. No one saw the athlete that existed inside me. That was apparent from my years in elementary.

I was usually last to be picked on a team, never passed the ball, etc. I didn't hear, "Great job on playing sports today." Never. But I certainly heard the teachers saying it to other students.

While no one saw that potential in me, I didn't step up to the plate either. I felt ashamed of myself and didn't connect well with others. I wasn't much of a team player.

The funny thing is that I am a full-time fitness professional and endurance athlete racing my mountain bike today. I play my sports with fire and passion. But this was an evolutionary stage that happened later in my life, which you will learn about soon.

Being in nature was where I got to be an athlete in my way. I played outside as often as possible throughout my school years. This is where I could escape, release, and gain control. It calmed me, so I developed a deep connection with the great outdoors.

But no matter what grade I was in, and still even now, paying attention and maintaining focus are two significant areas I need help with. When a sound trigger steals my focus and ignites emotions, it also instantly wipes my head of whatever thought or idea I had and takes over that space.

For example, I must re-read a paragraph if I am reading a book and then hear a sound. If I am doing math and then triggered, I will lose my spot in the problem-solving process and have to start over.

Quiet, please.
I can't get ahead.
I'm falling behind.

Panic. Anxiety.
Feeling like a dummy.
I don't care.

I'd feel incredibly defeated if I lost what I thought was an excellent idea. Sometimes I would quit or do a half-ass job to get it over with. It is mentally frustrating and exhausting to be interrupted repeatedly. It made me feel like a dummy, incapable of producing anything.

Writing this book, I have to wear earplugs even though I am all alone in my home. Beside me, I have a heater turned on. When the fan moves in one direction, it makes a clicking sound. Hearing that repeatedly steals my mind from my work. Earplugs go in. I need peace.

But I now know I have misophonia. I didn't know in school and I didn't have earplugs either. I had nothing. Daydreaming and disruptive behaviour was how I would cope while trying to flush the mean thoughts I had stirred up in my mind.

I knew I wasn't dumb. There were grand ideas in my head. I was curious and could solve problems, write, create, and express myself.

However, I couldn't get the information out of my head and into a final product because the pathway was constantly interrupted. I wished I could reach my hand into my head, grab my thoughts, and plop them onto a piece of paper.

Teachers are supposed to help students learn, but how can a teacher help a student who struggles without understanding the cause of that struggle? And clearly, most of them didn't care anyway. That may sound terrible, but it's how I felt.

They never asked me why I was acting the way I did. All they did was write notes on my report card. They offered no help to me. No teacher reached out. They ignored me.

When teachers would try to help me with my studies, it felt like I was being tortured. As they stood over me by my desk, their very presence and any sound they made would throw me off. I would freeze up, get confused, and then panic. Teachers intimidated me.

They would point out my mistakes, sending me off the rails. "I fucking know. I'm not stupid. Leave me the hell alone," is what I wanted to say. Instead, I had to agree, stay calm, and wait for them to move on to someone else.

I have always had a tough time receiving feedback from a teacher, my parents, or even a friend. I was not willing to admit fault, and I would twist things and blame everyone else for my behaviour.

I wanted to be alone, hide in a corner with a wall around me and be left alone to do my work. My inability to focus is everyone else's fault. The world is against me. I will resist you all. This is how I thought back in the day...

No wonder teachers didn't reach out to help me. I was resistant. It takes a lot of extra mental work to try and help someone, especially when that someone is unclear about why they behave the way they do.

After graduating, I continued to take courses and learned trades. I earned diplomas in bookkeeping, entrepreneurship, and computers. Now I'm learning beside other adults. It was challenging.

Sometimes I came off as grumpy for no reason. I'd snip at them. I hated how I made them feel, but I struggled to stop myself from acting that way. It felt compulsive.

At 30 years old, I decided to fulfill my childhood dream of becoming a schoolteacher. Funny how I wanted to get into the career that would put me back in a place where I had been tortured by so many sound triggers and bad memories. But I didn't think about it like that.

I was driven by the thought of producing an exciting learning environment for my students so they could feel comfortable and learn. I didn't even care what subject I taught. I just wanted to give them what I didn't have.

So off I went to Acadia University, embarking on a new chapter of my life. Now I was in the academic arena of higher education. There will be no moving about my seat, disrupting class, or any of those shenanigans. I had to control my emotions and behaviour better, including facial expressions and body language. It was serious now.

I was happy to discover that the classrooms were much more comfortable and sound-friendly. Some had theatre seating, soft carpet, comfy chairs, and better lighting. They were cozier all around.

I didn't have to sit in the same seat in every class. I could choose a seat away from a student who made sounds or move to a quieter corner of the room.

I was curious to hear every word the professors said. And...best of all...I was given a laptop, so I could stay focused by typing every word they would say...and that I did. I have entire course manuscripts of almost every word the professors would say, even the 'umms' and 'ahhs.' It saved me.

I put myself through university. My parents didn't pay for it. I wanted to squeeze everything I could out of this experience. I had to find a way to get through every day, every class, and that I did. I was learning ways to cope better because I was driven with an intention and purpose that set my soul on fire.

Going to university was one of the best things I ever did for myself. For the first time in my life, I felt compelled to get a grasp on my behaviour and attitude. Unknowingly, I began to "treat" myself. I still had all the emotions, but I was learning to channel them and distract myself.

There was only one big problem, though – exam rooms! The exam rooms were supposed to be quiet, but this was the loudest place ever for me. They were often held in the big gym.

As I walked toward the exam room, my heart pounded and trembled. It was the worst kind of torture because I knew what was coming, and I had to sit through it as my future depended on it.

Every time someone moved a chair, clicked a pen, sniffed, coughed, snapped gum, breathed loudly, shuffled paper...

Every little sound meant I had to start over. The battle inside my mind and body was lit.

Focus, Tammy. Tune it out. Get the idea out fast. Hurry up. Write it down. Ignore the outside. Stay inside your mind. For the love of God...STAY INSIDE YOUR MIND! You want this more than anything. You can do this. YOU CAN DO THIS!

The more intensely I need to concentrate, the more I am affected by sounds. They become more prominent, and the battle rages hotter.

Math has always been my nemesis. I know I can do it. I am good at it. But I failed at it so often. I struggled to hang on long enough to solve the problems. But if I had the right environment to work in, I would be like a human calculator.

But in university, I wanted something better than a C in math, the average grade I got throughout public school. I wanted an A+.

We were given three hours to write our math exams. It took me the entire three hours, and it was one big shit show in my head.

I fought hard against every noise and fought back the tears to keep pushing through. This was a battle I was determined to win.

When I finally turned in my exam and walked out the door, tears filled my eyes as I made my way to the car. I opened the door, sat in my seat, put my trembling hands on the steering wheel, and didn't move. My face was beet red.

I sat there for probably 10 minutes or more. I just started crying, trying to get it all out of me. I was shaking all over. My head was pounding. I felt like I just went through a war.

I commuted a long way to attend university, from the south shore to the valley. The drive one way took an hour and twenty minutes. I was thankful that day for the distance I had to travel. I put on some music and escaped the whole way home.

When I arrived, I was exhausted. Mentally and physically. I don't recall how the rest of my day went, but I know it was impacted just like every other time.

Exams were a required part of my educational journey. I had to do them, but they were my most significant obstacles. I eventually earned two degrees over six years.

That's many exams and a lot of unbelievable battles. But I won every single one of them. I graduated among the top in my class, received dozens of scholarships, and even made the Dean's list.

In my final year of university, I discovered that I had misophonia. I will tell you the story about that soon. But, one of my professors told me I could have had a quiet room set up for me to take my exams and study.

If only I had known.
If only I had known all my life.

I often wonder how different my life would have been if I had been given quiet learning spaces. I feel robbed of opportunities for extracurricular activities and social experiences. Thirteen years of my school life was mostly a waste.

But going to university made up for much knowledge I didn't get during my younger years. And I didn't stop there either. I continue my learning journey. Writing this book is part of that.

Since the discovery, I now know what I need to learn better. It has become a much more enjoyable and exhilarating experience.

I hope this chapter is read by teachers and educators because there will be young children, teens, and adults in their classrooms who knowingly or unknowingly have misophonia.

And some of them who know they have misophonia won't always speak up. It's hard to talk about when you feel no one understands. The additional stress is mentally and emotionally taxing. You get tired of it and find it easier to remain silent.

We need a greater understanding.
We need compassion and genuine support.
We need people to hear us and believe what we are saying.

CHAPTER 6: RELATIONSHIPS ARE HARD

"You're fucked."

Most of my boyfriends didn't understand, and my demands didn't help.

"Stop breathing so heavily."
"Go blow your nose."
"Why are you eating so loud?"
"Please stop making that tapping noise."

In most of my relationships, we didn't have excellent communication to begin with. Disrespectful and often littered with lies.

Complaining about sounds made me look crazy and led to additional friction.

One guy I dated often had to sleep on the couch because he snored. I also couldn't cuddle with him unless he quieted his breathing. We were both annoyed by this.

I screened men during dates to see how many sounds they made. They had to be under a certain threshold. Otherwise, it was not gonna happen.

I didn't care what they offered me. They could have been the kindest and most remarkable men in the world. Still, if they constantly triggered me, there was no relationship potential.

At 39 years old, I was a single mom, happily living alone with my son for roughly seven years. And then, one day, the kindest and most wonderful man in the world walked into my life - Justin.

He swept me off my feet, and he was a low trigger. That doesn't sound very romantic, but for me, he was a dream come true.

It was the first time in my life that I could talk to my partner about my sound triggers and wasn't called crazy or fucked up in the head.

While taking a road trip during the early stages of our relationship, he was tapping his fingers to music on the steering wheel. I asked him if he could stop. Of course, he seemed perplexed. I explained...

"There's something I need to tell you. I have this thing called misophonia."

He hadn't heard of it before. I explained some more. It was hard for him to understand. Most people have a hard time wrapping their heads around it. The reaction was typical.

"But I am enjoying the music. Tapping expresses that."

"I know, but that doesn't make my miso disappear."

It took a bit of coaching to get him to understand, and he will only partially get it. No one fully understands unless they have this disorder. I sent him some links to learn more, trying to back up my truth. He was receptive. He loved me. He respected me. And he cared.

Cooperating with compassion was vital. We had to bend together. We have found ways to live with my misophonia. Ten years later, here we still are.

As mentioned earlier, Justin is the one that planted the seed in my head to write a book about my experiences with misophonia.

I can't even explain how huge this is to me to have a compassionate, supportive partner. I don't fight him on it. He helps me with it. He never intentionally does anything to trigger me or use it against me.

Respectful communication, including tone of voice and word choices, has been one of our relationship's most profound and empowering features that keep us bonded. The relationship we have is a rare kind, and we both know it. We don't want to lose it. It takes work, and it's worth it.

Now, when it comes to relationships with friends, I have often struggled, which you have learned by now from previous stories I told.

Everyone makes noises. Some people make a lot more than others. When I decide to become closer to someone, I have to consider how much noise they make.

However, I can still become close to someone but physically distanced, and that's how I can maintain connections with those that often trigger me.

Ugh. I hate talking about this, but I know it's essential to help people understand why someone with misophonia may struggle to make or hang on to some relationships.

This is why I had very few or no close friends most of my life. Even unknowingly having misophonia, I'd rather be alone than sit next to someone triggering me, no matter how much I liked them.

Family, co-workers, clients, students...triggers exist in all of them. It didn't help that I constantly carried around a pocket full of anger. I was easily set off.

"You're behaviour is chaotic."
"You're too intense."
"You're so sensitive."

People find it challenging to be around me. Relationships are hard.

I mentioned my physical battles at school and home, but they didn't end there. As much as I hate to say this out loud and tell the world about it because it's incredibly embarrassing, I was physically violent up until my mid-30s.

I sometimes struggled to communicate my feelings and control my anger in social situations, especially when drinking. I got into fights at the bar and house parties.

This is violence and abuse. I abused people, people I didn't know, and people I loved dearly.

And I abused myself too. I hit my head, banged it into walls, slammed pillows, and sliced up my wrists twice. The slice was a cry for help, but no one even cared. Because I was a mean person?

I was seeking attention. I didn't want to die. I was abusing myself as a way to express my feelings that I did not know how to talk about.

I was fucked up. My behaviour could change instantly.

"What just happened? What is wrong with you?"

I often was called psycho. I tried to fight that label. Sometimes I'd ask myself, "Are you going crazy? Is this who you truly are?"

Having a stable relationship with anyone was hard AF! I screamed and yelled at my friends, boyfriends, parents...my son. My heart fills with shame admitting all of this.

Being pregnant for nine months and then breastfeeding for ten months meant that for the first time in many years, I had gone without alcohol or drugs. My head cleared up, but I did not like what was surfacing.

At age 22 and my son a few months old, I decided it was time to get therapy. The choice was driven by other reasons too, not just anger and depression. I was sexually abused as a child and teen. That is another story for another time. But it was time to deal with all of it.

Having my son was one of the best things that ever happened to my life, but at the same time, I found my mind going to dark places. Sober, with a beautiful son and wanting to be a good mom, I began to face my demons.

Finding the right therapist was hard. I had to jump around a bit, but I began to unravel and rebuild myself when it happened. This was the beginning of another road I realized I had to travel. I travelled it for the next 18 years.

I became more outraged and emotional while travelling that road. Still screaming. Still violent. More than ever.

I was mad at what I was uncovering and discovering. I was holding grudges and lashing back. It makes sense why I remained angry for so long.

Through most of my years in therapy, I still did not know I had misophonia. I mainly discussed my demons but never my relationships with sound, except this one time...

On my journey to finding the right therapist, I decided to try a psychiatrist. In our first and only session, this was the first time I mentioned how the sound of someone chewing gum made me instantly angry.

She responded, "I can help you with that." I sat up straight when she said it thinking, "This is a thing that can be helped?"

This would have been around 1995. Misophonia was coined in 2001. She knew something, but I didn't go back. That was it.

That was the only time during therapy that I ever talked about a sound and how it made me feel. I never brought it up in the other sessions. I was focused more on dealing with other trauma and figuring myself out.

My priority was developing a better relationship with myself to be a good mom and get through this life without being angry.

It was not easy. Not one little bit. And just because I was in therapy didn't mean I was on my way to a better place in a fast and furious manner. It doesn't work like that. I went off the rails many times. I hit rock bottom in the years to come when I went through a separation and financial destruction.

But I held on. Somehow, I managed to push through. I had to keep doing therapy. It was an 18-year rollercoaster ride that I couldn't get off of until I met the man of my dreams in 2012.

Mom says to me, "He fixed you." Happy tears, and sad tears, because she's right. He kinda did fix me. What really happened was that he helped me to fix myself. He gave me what no one else could. He allowed me to be myself, listened closely to what I wanted in myself, and then supported me in the way I needed so I could make shit happen.

And I can't finish this chapter without saying this...

The strength I gathered to get help and start the journey towards fixing myself, I also owe to my parents. Not because they always helped me, as there were plenty of times I wouldn't let them, but because they always believed in me. No matter how much of an ass I was, how angry and hateful I became, and all the mean things I said and did, they knew I had something special inside me. But I couldn't see it until I was ready to see it.

My mom always said, "My dear daughter, you'll find what you seek."

She's right. Once I decided to seek peace within and a better understanding of myself, I could finally find what I had been looking for all my life.

CHAPTER 7: I LOST MY MOM

Now, this is where it gets hard to write my story...

I lost my mom, and I let it happen. I made it happen.

Mom was and still is on my high-trigger list. This breaks my heart to say it out loud, and because I know she is reading these words, they are probably tearing her up inside.

It doesn't mean I don't love her. I find it hard to be around her because of the sounds I hear and the emotional response they create. If you took those sounds she made and made them someone else's, I would feel the same. It's not my mom. It's the sounds.

But I didn't know that growing up. I blamed Mom for the way I felt. She caused it by making all those sounds. I didn't know it was misophonia, and the medical term didn't even exist back then. I thought it was her.

And I often felt it was deliberate and that she could stop making those sounds. I kept that thought in my mind, but acted out by releasing my frustration toward her. No wonder she didn't understand me.

Mom and I have been through too much, together and apart. We struggled to develop a secure and loving mother-daughter relationship. For almost 40 years, we were at war. My misophonia played a significant role. It fueled the constant battle between us. My behaviour was hurtful. I let it all happen.

Growing up, I HATED being around my mother, yet I wanted so badly to be around her. Hate is a terrible feeling, but it's how I felt. This is hard to admit, and tears fill my eyes as I write this. It was the reality, and I now need to tell my truth because someone else reading this may experience the same situation.

Being around my mother felt like I was being tortured. The sounds she made were constant, never-ending...I can still hear them in my head. I knew they were coming before I even heard them. Spending any time near her making those sounds drove me crazy.

These were normal sounds to everyone else in the house. No one else even noticed. But for me, it was like having my raging emotions on repeat. And naturally, no one knew what was wrong with me. So, I was deemed a hateful, hard-to-be-around person. I was the mean black sheep of the family.

I grew to hate my mother, even though I loved her. Yes, this is possible. I felt the sounds were "training" me to feel hate frequently. It was not an uncommon emotion for me. But I loved her so much, and so it was an actual form of a love-hate relationship. Not a terrific way to grow up.

I was often disgusted, especially when it came to her eating, breathing, and biting her nails. I could barely sit in the same room with her without blowing up. I'd rather be in my room or outside. I would try to spend time with her when I was having a good day, but it would rarely go how I wanted it to. She would make a sound, and I would flip out.

It often ended in a fight. Mom had no idea what she did or why I would turn on her. It created an enormous amount of friction and tension between us. She felt the hate and disgust. I didn't hold it back. I wore on the outside what I was feeling inside.

I would try again and again to be with her. It was a tiring rollercoaster ride at times because I wanted so badly to have a loving and caring relationship with her. I wanted to sit with her and talk, get advice, do things with her, be best friends, wrap my arms around her and tell her how much I love her.

But we didn't have that.
We had the opposite of that.

Even watching TV together, I couldn't sit near her on the couch. I would always lay on the floor close to the TV as possible and use the TV sounds to drown out hers.

I would cup my hand over my ear on the side I was lying on, but I still had the issue of the other ear being exposed. So, I would use the top of my shoulder to tuck my earlobe into my ear and lay my top arm over my head.

It was very uncomfortable, but I didn't care because the pain of hearing her sounds was worse than the pain of being uncomfortable.

It didn't last long. I'd watch the show and then go to my room. I snipped Mom off if she asked me anything during this time. My voice generally carried a hateful tone.

I couldn't stand it. I fucking hated it. I fucking hate even remembering this. My heart is pounding right now.

I was around 14 years old, sitting on the couch one evening, listening to my cousin play guitar as my mom sang. She was sitting on the living room floor in front of me.

Mom could sing like an angel. I loved hearing her voice. It was soothing. It would sweep me away. The perfect tone and flow of sounds from the lyrics she sang. She gave me goosebumps.

After singing one of her songs, out of the blue, she tried to talk to me about my attitude. She had a few drinks, so she felt relaxed about bringing it up.

"What am I doing that you hate me so much?"

She went on and on, and I just sat there looking at her, listening and didn't say a thing. The more she talked, the angrier I got. Inside my head was this: "You're disgusting."

How do you tell your mom that her presence drives you insane because she makes the most annoying and grotesque sounds every day of your life? You don't. But it was what I wanted to say.

And I didn't understand what the hell was wrong with me, so how do I put something like that into words?

Instead of talking, I stormed off to my room. All I wanted to do was listen to Mom sing. I was pissed. I remember feeling like she ruined my evening. She took away my peace and calm.

Mom and I fought over everything.

Mom: "Let me teach you how to cook."

Me: "I don't plan to make the types of food you do."

Mom: "And what types of food is that?"

Me: stomps off to my room

My mom was a fantastic cook, and I missed an incredible

opportunity to learn her craft. But as I said many times, I couldn't stand being near her for any length of time.

Add the sounds of clanging dishes, pots and pans, and other kitchen noises to the mix... I would be an absolute mess. There's no learning happening. I can't pay attention. All I want to do is fight, scream, yell, pull my hair out, and bang my head against a wall.

A few times, we would try, and when I would ask again for an explanation, the reaction was, "you're not listening to me," which made me feel stupid.

She was right. I wasn't listening. I was too busy trying to battle the rage inside me, so I could do the thing she wanted me to do, but inside me, the emotions were building to high intensity. I would get so confused and frustrated. I would then act out, treating her like it was all her fault.

This broke her heart. She wanted to teach me basic skills parents usually teach their children, and I shot it all down. I didn't let her be my mother.

Years later, when I discovered my misophonia and reflected on my life, I saw how badly this impacted me after I left home. She was trying to teach me the very things I needed.

It was a disaster. It was always like this. My mom couldn't teach me anything. We couldn't talk. We could not go anywhere together. It was always a fight.

As a little girl with long hair, sometimes she would French braid it. I would sit there, listening to her breathe the whole time. I'm holding my hands, rubbing them together, squeezing my fists, pulling on my fingers, just waiting for it to be over.

By the end, I was burning up inside. I would go to my room and get all the emotions out, screaming into my pillow, cupping my ears, and trying to get the sound out of my head.

I wanted my mom to braid my hair. I wanted to feel her fingers through my hair, listen to her stories, and spend time with her. I know she enjoyed it too. But I would get anxious for her to be done.

"Do you want me to braid your hair or not?"

Mom wanted me to ask her for help. She tried to guide me through life. Feeling valuable and helpful are great feelings to have as a parent. I get it now. I'm a mom too. When your child asks you for help, no matter how old, they say they need you. It's a precious feeling.

Even though I wanted my mom's help, I didn't ever want her help, and I sure as hell let her know it most of my life. If she offered, I shut her down. I would get sour and mean. It never ended well. It was so hard. Our relationship was in constant turmoil.

Mornings, waiting for the bus in the living room, I could hear Mom getting out of bed, and I would immediately get angry. She was making her way downstairs to see me off for school. I would plug my ears until she was visible in the room.

I would have loved to have a morning chat with my mom and set up my day, but instead, I would cringe at the thought of the sounds that were about to happen. Rage and disgust were already bubbling inside me.

She used to be a heavy smoker. First, I could hear her coughing and gagging. Then I could hear her feet scuffing the floor as she moved towards the steps, followed by heavy breathing as she walked down the stairs and into the room.

There, I would stand with a hateful face. I couldn't even look at Mom. By this point, I was screaming inside. Heart pounding, head full of rage, thinking, "Why can't you just stay in bed." I even asked her this one time, and of course, she felt offended.

I'd stay in my room on weekends until she was up and about. Her breathing would settle as her body woke up. I never wanted to come out of my room anyway. It was the best room in the house.

Because I didn't understand so much about myself, I blamed everyone else and the world, and Mom was the easiest target of all. I abused her, and during all that time, I honestly felt like she was abusing me...with those damn sounds she was always making. She became my punching bag.

My dad was a fisherman and spent much of his life at sea. He didn't even see half of what went on between my mom and me, but he experienced enough to make him say I was "difficult to live with."

Dad made noises too, but I wasn't around him as much as my mother because of his job. He would pick his teeth after supper and suck air through them, making me cringe at every sound.

I'm not sure why I didn't go to therapy. I suppose during these days, therapy wasn't the first thing that came to mind to solving problems. Besides, I didn't know how to express what was wrong with me. How would therapy have helped?

When I finally left home at age 18, I felt like I was escaping dysfunction and turmoil. I was wrong. The dysfunction and disruption lived inside me. It travelled with me no matter where I went.

I often wonder how things would have turned out differently if I could have had a more loving and close relationship with my mother. She wanted to share her stories, ideas, and lessons, and I missed out on that. I'm sure she dreamed of a different type of relationship when I was born...

Your daughter is born. You hold her in your arms, sing to her, and watch her grow. As she grows, you are excited to teach her things to help her succeed. You develop a beautiful and nurturing, precious, heart-warming relationship.

Mom loves me with all her heart and soul. That's all she ever wanted to do. I wouldn't let her love me the way she wanted to.

That was a constant punch to her heart. Neither of us understood, and I couldn't talk to her about the real issues because I didn't know I had misophonia.

I know my mom loved me, but I'm sure there were many times she didn't like me very much. I know she could feel my anger and disgust toward her. As a parent, that's a hard pill to swallow.

As a mom, I can imagine how painful this was. And when we talk about it now, she brushes it off as a mother would, trying not to make her child feel bad...but I know our past relationship broke her heart and brought sadness into her soul.

It hurts so bad to admit to all of this.

But now we are here. Today. At this very moment, as I write these words, while I shed my tears, I can also smile. We both understand now. We are working to take back what was stolen from us during those 40 years of our lives.

Mom, I know you are reading this...

It's not your fault.
It wasn't you.
It was never you.

I'm so sorry I hurt you.

CHAPTER 8: I DON'T HATE YOUR DOG!

"I love it when your dog outside barks for what seems like forever," says no one, ever!

You don't even need to have misophonia to feel enraged by this. Most dog owners allow this to happen in all the places I have lived. It's inconsiderate. It interrupts the peace of our neighbourhoods and our personal lives.

Because dog sounds have climbed to the top of my trigger list over the past few years and have caused me great pain and suffering, I am giving this topic a chapter of its own. I feel highly misunderstood, even when I try to explain what is happening to me, especially to a dog owner.

And this chapter is risky to write. In revealing negative emotions about my experiences with dogs, some people will accuse me of being a dog hater. You might as well say I am an evil person.

But they are wrong.

I don't hate dogs! I have had dogs most of my life. I grew up with them at home and had two of my own later in life.

Mom and Dad had a dog named Charlie. Charlie was loud, and the sounds he made while in the house drove me nuts. I couldn't stand hearing him eat, lick, make mouth noises, his nails as he walked across the floor...

Charlie had a high-pitched bark. The longer he barked, the angrier I got. I felt compelled to stop the barking. I would do anything to make it stop.

One late night, Charlie started barking. It was pouring rain. His dog house was on the same side of the house as my bedroom. When he barked, it sounded like he was right outside my window.

He barked that high-pitch sound, and it went on and on. Nobody got up to see what was happening, so I went out, and there he was, tangled up in his chain. I had to get him untangled. We were both covered in mud.

Charlie stopped barking. We both settled down and went back to sleep, he in his dog house and I in my bed. But that barking sound and memory never faded away. I can still hear it. I can still feel it today.

I loved Charlie, but he drove me insane with his dog sounds. I swore to myself that I would never own a dog. When I was living out on my own, and after my son was born, I got a little dog. I know. Go figure.

Her name was Sunshine. She was adorable, tiny, and could sit on my shoulder. She loved me and followed me everywhere. We bonded. And yet, even this little, innocent dog made big sounds. It hurts to say this, but I punished her for making them.

I didn't allow her to chew on anything. If she licked her lips or made mouth sounds for a time that I felt was unnecessary, I silenced her by saying 'No.' She would look at me with those sad eyes before she walked away.

The fact that I could silence her made me happy because I felt in control. However, I couldn't teach her to stop barking. I didn't know how. If anyone came to the door, she would bark like crazy.

Most people found it funny, as she was this tiny dog with this big bark. The comedy of it all took the edge off a bit. I was able to calm her down but never got it under control. It was a challenge.

In owning a dog, I felt like I had more control over the sounds it would make. This is important for me with misophonia. Knowing I can stop a sound or even reduce its impact helps to relieve some of the panic and stress.

Commanding my dog is one thing, but commanding someone else's is another. That's like telling someone else's child how to behave right before the parent. You don't do that.

My first uncomfortable experience was when my neighbours across the street let their dog outside, and it would bark intermittently for hours. This was during a time when I didn't know I had misophonia.

I ran a home-based business. My office was in a cute, quiet attic space away from the rest of the house. Every time I heard that dog bark, the earplugs would go in, but I could still hear it bark. The sound echoed and felt like it was filling up every space inside my house. I could not get any relief.

I had a bookkeeping business. Managing someone's financial records, you want to ensure everything is recorded accurately. When my neighbour's dog started barking, I couldn't work. It was interfering with my business operations. I was beyond frustrated. I had to focus.

So, I wrote my neighbours a letter. It was a kindly-worded and respectful letter. I started by telling them how much I loved their dog. Then I explained how I struggled with the barking and how it impacted my life. I put the letter in their mailbox. I was shaking and sick to my stomach.

I lost sleep over this. I thought about it for a long time. Should I do this? Am I going to create a problem? Are they going to hate me? I knew my neighbours. Their son was in the same school grade as mine.

My neighbour called me. I was expecting an argument, but she was so sympathetic. We talked, and they agreed to do what they could to minimize the barking. They followed through. I am glad it turned out this way because it could have been ugly.

These happy endings are not typical for the most part. Most of the time, if I speak up, I get a negative and snarky reaction. People will say things like, "Dogs bark." I want to roll my eyes and say: "No. Really? Dogs bark? I never knew that."

Of course, I fucking know that dogs bark. Please don't say this when I am trying to delicately explain the rage that is brewing inside me. Making that kind of statement adds fuel to the fire already burning inside.

Knowing that dogs bark doesn't make my misophonia go away. It doesn't stop the emotional chain reaction. It's a trigger. It's uncontrollable!

That comment is degrading and shows a considerable lack of compassion. This is a prime example of people's reactions in general when I try to explain the impact specific sounds have on me, especially if it's coming directly from them or something related to them. They get defensive and treat me like I'm causing an abrasive situation.

When I knew I had misophonia, I was coaching a client in her home. She had a dog. It was in the same room with us, chewing on a bone. I couldn't focus on our discussion. In the middle of a sentence, I would lose my thoughts. There would be an awkward pause as I clenched my fists and moved around in my seat, trying to find a piece of comfort.

She is paying for my services. I must do a good job. But I could feel myself falling apart in a professional setting where I needed to keep my composure... and I couldn't stop it.

My expressions were shifting as I was getting squirmy in my seat, trying to figure out how to get through the rest of this session. I couldn't stop looking at my client's dog chewing on that damn bone. I can still hear it now. It still angers me.

She noticed the change in me and how I looked at her dog. Then she asked, "You don't like dogs?" I felt sick to my stomach. That's like asking, "You don't like my kid?" My heart sank.

She was a lovely woman. She wasn't just a client of mine. We had a personal working relationship. I also substitute taught in her classroom. I felt like I did something horrible to her. I feared what this would do to our relationship.

I tried to explain that dog sounds caused me to become frustrated. It was a very uncomfortable discussion because she had heard nothing like this. I didn't want to admit anything, but she needed to understand why I was awkward.

Even as a teacher, she wasn't aware that sounds could impact someone so intensely. It has been my experience that most teachers don't even know about misophonia, thus one reason I'm writing this book. It's a demand for greater awareness to be brought inside the school system as the kids with misophonia need the right kind of understanding and support. I don't want them to feel robbed of learning and social opportunities, as I experienced in my childhood.

She got up and put her dog outside to comfort me, but the tension in the room was not good. After this incident, our relationship was interrupted. I felt weird trying to explain, and I wasn't doing an outstanding job at that point. Still discovering the disorder, trying to understand how to put that in words... sometimes I would screw it up. Unfortunately, that was our last coaching session.

It never seemed to matter how strong of a relationship I thought I had with someone. For my misophonia, they did not perceive it as an actual disorder. Compassion was faked. Empathy was non-existent. People treated me like it was a personality problem and that my feelings were inconvenient.

My best friend of 20+ years had four dogs. She loved them, but like most dog owners I know, she didn't train them. It was like having four misbehaved children. I loved spending time with her and wanted that so badly. Therefore, I built a relationship with her dogs and loved them like my own.

They barked, especially the two little ones. I had to prepare myself for the visits, and thankfully, the barking would eventually simmer down. I got through it, and she would try to help. She even got a BarxBuddy, but it failed to work.

I told her about my misophonia. I talked to her openly about it. She knew very well how I struggled every single day. But I think she felt blame and responsibility, which I probably transferred in my tone and word choices. It's not all her fault. I will admit this.

One day, I faced a gut-wrenching discovery, at which point I realized that her compassion wasn't genuine. This also explained why her efforts to help me seemed half-assed, but I had already accepted that, even though it dug at me. I wanted to keep our relationship as I loved her so much.

She had a friend at her house whom I had never met before. I came for a visit to meet her. She stood there, watching me interact with the dogs. I greeted them like I usually would.

One dog would circle through my legs like he always did. The other would run away, hide, and act like he hated me. He did that to everyone. And there was the other little dog I called my spirit animal. I would get him all riled up. We would play right away. And the fourth dog would just lay on the floor and pop his head up. There were naps to be had.

Playing an active part with dogs helped me cope with my misophonia. It gave me a little sense of control and would tame the beast inside me. It's when I have no control whatsoever that everything gets amplified.

After a few moments, and the greetings started to wind down, her friend said, "I thought she hated dogs." I heard this loud and clear.

My heart sank. I could not believe what I had just heard. This is what my best friend, who is supposed to genuinely care for me, says to others behind my back? That I hate dogs? After all these years, after telling her at the deepest level what I'm going through in my mind, body, heart...

At that very moment, all the compassion I thought she had for my situation with misophonia vanished. It was fake. It was fucking fake. It wasn't real. It never was real. She had not heard a word I said all this time. She never sought to understand. She faked her sympathy.

At that moment, I lost all my trust. I could no longer talk about my misophonia. I felt utterly defeated. If I couldn't talk to my best friend and feel understood and supported, then who could I talk to? Thankfully, I did have others in my life, but this still was a kick in the teeth.

I don't hate dogs, but I do hate the sounds they make. I also hate how I am treated when I tell people what is happening inside me when I hear dog sounds.

As the years went by, the dog sound triggers worsened, likely due to the over-exposure. It can get so bad that I can't sit peacefully on my back deck on a sunny day. The continuous barking forces me back inside my house. Sometimes, I have to put loud music on, use earplugs, go to the basement, or leave my property and go somewhere else for a while.

Later in life, I moved to a different part of the country. I loved our new home and location within walking distance next to the trails. But, it was only a short time before I noticed a huge problem. Almost everyone in the neighbourhood had a dog, and most of them let their dog bark for what felt like hours.

I have had to call animal control on my neighbours more times than I would like to admit. I tracked each dog's barking time, duration, and location. According to the city's bylaw where we lived, dogs are not allowed to bark for more than five minutes at a time and intermittently throughout the day.

And so, it continued for years after. I kept a log. When I would drive by the home of the barking dog, I would jot down the house number. Sometimes I had to deliberately go out for a walk or ride around on my bike to collect house numbers.

Animal control officers were receptive. I reported the dogs on a quarterly to bi-annual basis. I was even told that they get high incident reports for my neighbourhood. Some of the dogs were aggressive too.

I was like, "bring it on" for summer and winter because there was less barking during these times. People would keep their dogs inside. During the summer, people left on vacations. It can get sweltering hot, so the dogs would be brought inside. For winter, people would also bring their dogs inside during the frequent frigid temps and cold snaps.

During spring and fall? BRUTAL! Unbelievably brutal. This was when I made the majority of my reports. The animal control officers would go to their houses and talk with the owners. Then they would call me back and let me know the status. Most times, the owners were compliant, but only for a little while. Every season, I'd have to go through the same process.

And now and then, you'd have that neighbour who didn't care. It got to the point that if I wanted to stop their dog from barking so much, I was told I would have to take my neighbour to court. I do not wish to take someone to court for a barking dog. What a way to cause division among neighbours.

However, I will talk in this book about it and hopefully create a positive understanding, encouraging dog owners to be more aware of the impact their barking dog can have on others in their community.

I know many others with misophonia are going through this experience. Two of my friends admitted that they had to sell their homes and move to another neighbourhood due to the same issues I had experienced. I am not standing alone on this important matter. It's a real problem.

After several years of living in that neighbourhood, and for other reasons, we sold our house and transitioned to full-time RV living. We have a home base at an RV park. I was thrilled to learn they have a no-bark rule. I have peace and quiet and can sit in my backyard for hours. It is wonderful.

Every time we travel with our RV, I'm worried. Not all campgrounds or RV parks have no-bark rules. I check their guides. I scope things out and get more isolated sites. It is disheartening to escape to a place where I hope for quiet, only to be tortured by barking dogs.

I have become so incredibly sensitized to dog sounds that they trigger me with great intensity in less than a second. The sounds can echo. I feel like they are piercing my brain. I fall apart so quickly as the rage soars higher with every second that goes by. It is clear why they have made it at the top of my severe trigger list.

It's an ongoing struggle, and it's a big one. For the most part, I have no control over the dogs, and I can't make it stop.

And again, as weird as this may sound with all that I have said...

I do not hate your dog!

I hate the sounds your dog makes. There's a difference.

The end.

CHAPTER 9: THE DAY I DISCOVERED I WASN'T CRAZY

At age 37, my life changed in one moment.

I was studying to become a schoolteacher at Acadia university. While sitting in an inclusive education class, the professor discussed hearing disorders in children.

As she moved through various conditions, she talked about how the brain can misinterpret certain words and sounds. A person then can experience sudden confusion, panic, anger, embarrassment, fear, etc.

As she continued talking more, I sat straight up in my chair. A rush went through my body. My heart was pounding, and my mind was lit.

After class, I hung back and told my professor a little about what certain sounds do to me. This was the first time I ever heard the word 'misophonia.'

As I stood there, listening to her explain the condition, I started to cry. I was shaking. She hugged me. She told me there was help for me. We talked for a while.

This was the moment my life changed.

All these years...all the suffering in silence...the pain, the thoughts in my head about myself, the confusion, the embarrassment, the shame...

I'm not a hateful person.
There's a reason for my rage.
This is real, and I'm not the only one suffering.

Finally, I could seek to understand.

The first thing I did was Google it. I read personal blogs and also found websites on misophonia.

I diagnosed myself and found validation. I said in my head, "This is me. This is how I feel. This is what I have."

I did a presentation on misophonia in our inclusive education course. I gathered my resources, put my slides together, and spoke in front of the class.

I had to fight the tears. It was emotional. I stood there in front of my peers, explaining my life but also not explaining my life. I was there to create awareness and to inform them it was an actual disorder, what it does and how it impacts someone, and that about 2% of their students could have it.

Everything I mentioned in the chapters about my childhood was popping into my head as I tried to teach. All the struggles I had as a student were flashing through my mind. I remembered the times a teacher told me to stop daydreaming, the sadness of feeling alone, and how awkward and weird I always felt.

It was clear to the students and the professor that my lesson was based on my story and not just on scientific information. But I didn't expect what would happen afterwards.

After hearing my presentation, two peers told me they might also have misophonia. They did not know it was a thing.

I cried.

For the first time in my life, I met people with a similar sound rage that I have. At that moment, I truly knew that I wasn't alone. I felt the possibility that many more of us in the room have it but were scared to talk about it.

How many people have misophonia? We don't know exactly how many because it's tough to talk about, and for sad reasons. What happened after my discovery made me wish I had never discovered it.

When I learned and self-diagnosed myself as having misophonia, I immediately told my family, starting with my mom. I couldn't wait to talk to her because I felt I had validation of my behaviour all these years.

"See, Mom, this has been going on with me. I wasn't a hateful snip."

"OMG," she said. "It all makes so much sense now."

We talked for a while, bringing up memories and having so many "ah" moments. Mom even told me things I didn't remember, such as the backseat car story with my brother breathing loudly. We now make jokes about that. We didn't know then, but we know now.

But unfortunately, as I told others, I felt more ashamed than ever before. I began to regret my discovery. Was I better off not knowing that I have misophonia? Was I better off keeping it a secret and living in silent suffering?

When I tried to explain my condition, I felt no one believed me. People's reactions made me feel like a whacko and that it was all in my head. Some people rolled their eyes or told me to "just deal with it." Some made snarky comments like, "just block it out."

No one was willing to work with me. People didn't like to be told that they were making a sound that bothered me. They didn't want to change their behaviours to accommodate my problems.

My co-worker whistled at work. My boyfriend still breathed loudly. My mom continued to chew gum while I visited.

I compare it to a person in a wheelchair.

Imagine rolling up to someone. The wheelchair is visible. You don't have to explain. Then you are told that the wheelchair is unfounded and you should "just get up and walk."

They aren't willing to offer any support or assistance to help you out, so you can live a better life. They label you and treat you like a lesser person, like you are mentally incapable, or weaker, or fucked up...or faking it.

With misophonia, I have to tell people that I have something invisible. You may see me acting weird with a switch in behaviour and attitude, but you won't know it's due to this disorder unless I explain.

But when I tell people, they still think I have complete control over it and can walk it off. They don't stop the noise or try to accommodate me to make me feel more comfortable. Instead, they often roll their eyes or get an expression of disbelief on their face. It makes me feel worse than I already do.

I operated a fitness studio on the bottom level of my home. On the way was a poster asking clients and students to refrain from making several noises that significantly triggered me. I would also send out an email to my clients and students as a friendly reminder before showing up for classes.

On the list were the following sounds: grunting or clanking weights on each rep, Ujjayi breathing, sucking on candy or lozenges, eating during instruction, pen clicking, and chewing gum.

On one particular occasion, a client showed up with gum in her mouth. I asked her to spit it out.

"It helps with my anxiety," she said.

I pointed to my poster and replied with a gut-wrenching feeling in my stomach that I even had to do this right now...

"I'm sorry. Gum chewing is a severe trigger, and I won't be able to coach you."

The expression on her face... Not a word was said. She spits the gum into her hand and throws it in the trash.

I said, "thank you." She said nothing. I could feel the tension. It wasn't a great way to start a personal coaching session. Yuck.

We started, the tension disappeared, and we got through the session. But after my client left, I cried. I felt terrible. I hated every fucking moment of that whole scene. I was putting my misophonia above her anxiety. But I didn't know what else to do. If I let her chew the gum, the session could not continue.

This situation ruined the rest of my day, not just because of the gum chewing but because of a more profound reason that lives in my heart and soul.

I have been working in the fitness industry since 1999. When I started teaching classes under my operations, I wanted to set the bar higher by creating a comfortable and accepting atmosphere for everyone that joined me.

I provide services that can become very personal and meaningful to some individuals, which hits on some sensitive areas. This requires a lot of compassion and empathy. I'm not just a fitness trainer and educator. I'm a mentor and a leader. People look to me for personalized guidance on deep, meaningful goals that will change their lives.

When an awkward situation arises from my misophonia, I struggle hard because I do not want any client or student to feel bad. And I certainly don't want them to make any sacrifices to accommodate my disorder.

But the fact is this - there's no way around it. I can't help what it does to me, and there are certain sounds that I can't cope with. The sound must stop altogether, or I must leave the area. There's no other option. Not even earplugs, especially when it involves sight and sound. I can't coach or teach with my eyes and ears shut.

Explaining my misophonia to clients and students has sometimes been highly challenging. More so than trying to explain to a friend.

I am passionate about my career and what I provide for people. It's genuine, and you will learn why it has a deeper meaning to me later in this book.

Over the years, I have become angrier and even more frustrated with my misophonia. I wished I had never discovered it, never had to know about it, talk about it, or explain it to anyone while feeling shame and disbelief and experiencing those god-awful situations. It seemed to disrupt my life more than ever since knowing I had it.

I joined some Facebook groups in my search to discover ways to cope and hear other people's stories. The first group I joined was a place of rants. That was a huge eye-opener.

"Do I sound like that when I talk about my misophonia to other people?"

Full of blame? Ripping others apart? Showing little responsibility for my behaviour? Using it as a scapegoat? Avoiding the work I needed to do to help myself live a better life with misophonia? And...

Expecting the world to change.
Expecting people to instantly understand me.
Expecting everyone to accommodate my misophonia.

The longer I was in that group, the more I realized I was thinking, behaving, and communicating like this. I wanted to come across differently.

I began to notice that my ranting and blaming were fueling the fire, making everything feel worse. I checked the group daily and eventually realized how it negatively impacted my thoughts for the rest of that day. It shows how important it is to surround yourself with the right vibe if you want to strive towards happiness within yourself. So, I left the group.

And honestly, there was one big positive I did take from being in this group. It made me reflect on my behaviour. I blamed, ranted, accused, fought, and made others feel like they were causing my pain. This may be where I could have done better. This may be my issue.

This very light bulb moment is where the real journey began toward a better understanding of my misophonia, specifically the "living with it." I needed to learn to talk about my misophonia without making others feel they were to blame for my pain and suffering. Instead of telling them what they need to do, I need to work on what I need to do to live with it.

I was filled with hurt and anger when I started talking about it. I felt that I had justification for my behaviour. I wanted to release the pent-up feelings I had kept quiet about for decades. It felt freeing, but in doing so, I came across as blaming everyone and the world.

When I told my mom about it, I can clearly remember the

thoughts in my head about how my words were delivering the underlying message...

"I wasn't a hateful snip, Mom. You were making sounds that triggered me to behave that way. My behaviour is now validated."

And I am sure Mom's heart sank, and I didn't even know it because I was wrapped up in myself again. Her heart was already torn from all those hard years trying to raise me. Now she felt the added responsibility for my misophonia because of how I delivered the news to her.

God almighty. This tears me up inside.

I longed to be heard and understood, but I was hurting others while telling my story, trying to explain what was wrong with me.

Even though I left that Facebook group, it was one of the best things I found in the journey to learn about misophonia. It made me look in the mirror. I did not like what I saw.

If I ever wanted to be heard, understood, and supported, I had to find a better way to behave and communicate about my misophonia.

Now, I was no longer just challenged by sounds. I needed to develop personalized coping mechanisms to live without feeling trapped by typical everyday sounds.

And I also needed to find peace within, learn how to protect it with confidence, and stand up for myself in a non-blaming and negative way.

I had to let go of feeling ashamed. That was, and still is, a struggle.

These challenges will never end. It is a daily quest for acceptance...

The world would not change for me. I was the one who had to change... for me. And part of that change is writing this book.

CHAPTER 10: THE "DIAGNOSIS"

In 2015, about six years after discovering misophonia, I pursued a medical assessment. There is no formal assessment or protocol to diagnose misophonia. Regardless, I wanted a medical evaluation and a doctor's opinion for two reasons.

First, I wanted something that I could use as "proof" to back up and validate my explanation when speaking to people who didn't believe me. I use this now when I often talk about the disorder to someone who has never heard of it to establish credibility.

"It's a real thing. I had a medical evaluation."

Second, I needed validation for myself. Every day, I asked myself, "What is wrong with me?" That question becomes mentally unhealthy when repeated repeatedly. I needed something to help me change the way I speak to myself.

I made an appointment with my family doctor and felt surprised he knew of misophonia. He referred me to a hearing specialist.

The specialist had a degree in neurology. I don't remember his name, but he knew much more about misophonia than my family doctor did.

I felt in excellent hands. I felt excited too. People were listening to me, and they were experts.

First, I had a hearing test. The specialist found my left ear to be "supersonic," above average hearing. My right ear was less than 100%, but still good. Nothing to worry about at this time.

Then I had a CT scan for structural damage, and it came up clean. Sometimes sounds can be amplified off of bone structures, so it made sense to see if something was out of the ordinary.

Then there was the interview after all the tests. I was asked a series of questions to learn more about what I was experiencing, specifically what sounds bothered me and how I reacted to them.

Also, we talked about how this impacted my life. It was a reasonably thorough discussion, and I felt comfortable opening up. The specialist showed me that he took this seriously and listened carefully to what I was saying. I felt safe.

After the entire evaluation was complete, based on all the data, he concluded that I indeed have misophonia. He explained that misophonia impacts how the brain interprets certain sounds. The brain interprets a typical, non-threatening sound as a threat. That's why I experience a fight, flight or freeze response. That's where my extreme emotions come from.

There is no “cure" at the moment. The cause is still unknown. Even though the specialist knew about misophonia, he indicated that there was still much to learn, as it was a relatively new discovery.

I asked him more questions. Then we talked about coping mechanisms. I could take medications to calm the anxiety. He also suggested cognitive therapy using sound exposure to try to remap the interpretation by the brain.

I didn't do either. I never had the money for the therapy. Looking back at my misophonia development, I'm not feeling confident about the success of sound exposure as a form of treatment, considering my discovery that over-exposure heightens the emotional response.

And I prefer to find natural alternatives to taking medications, which I did find. They are the coping mechanisms I developed for myself. I will share this in later chapters.

Also, I want to mention something I noticed since the "diagnosis." Sometimes I feel that knowing I have misophonia makes it worse. I'm more aware of my triggers, and sometimes I catch myself tuning into sounds by choice. Usually, the sound would come to me, not the other way around.

I get worried. I have so many questions I still need to answer. Some of them I am scared to ask...

Am I training my brain to be more heightened and sensitive?
Is this why it's getting worse?
Is this why I am accumulating more triggers?
Am I thinking my misophonia worse?
Is misophonia tied to emotional trauma?
Can the brain's interpretation of these triggers be remapped?

Regardless of all the things I have yet to learn, I'm lucky to have seen medical professionals that allowed me to go through this process and receive the validation and help I needed. This set me on a new path to learning how to understand this disorder and what I need to do to live with it better.

Now I have a new doctor. He had never even heard of misophonia. I had to inform him what it was. It's 2022. I hear the same thing when I share my story with others who have misophonia. The medical community at large is still very unaware of misophonia. This book will help to change that. There are people out there that need professional help.

Misophonia is real. It is a disorder. And here I am, living with it and writing a book about that. No, I can't control it, but I can do this...

Explore better ways to communicate about it.
Stop placing blame on others and the world around me.
Develop better coping mechanisms and behaviours.
Seek a more calm and peaceful way to live my life.
Learn how to forgive myself and move on.
Create more awareness and help others.

Over the following few chapters, I will touch on the above list and share what I have learned, accomplished, and still need to work on.

One thing is for sure, this journey has no destination. It's a path I will travel for the rest of my life. I know that even after this book is done and published, I will still be developing systems for better communication, coping, and escaping the sound traps to protect my peace.

I have accepted that.
I have no other choice.

CHAPTER 11: COMMUNICATION IS KEY

Communicating about something I didn't know I had was not possible. I couldn't find the words because I didn't understand what was happening inside me. How do you make the connections and then explain them to others? I didn't.

On the day of discovery, starting with that moment in the Acadia classroom, my mind was lit, making uncountable connections as the memories came rushing in.

I told people, "See, this is why I am the way I am." Then I blamed the world and everyone for it.

Why did I take that approach?

I grew up in a family that was very loving and compassionate. Still, we often argued when we disagreed. There was lots of yelling and screaming, combined with an abrasive tone of voice, words of friction, blame, assumptions, and so on. No one is to blame. We all took part.

I needed better communication skills. In school, I struggled to get my ideas out and to be understood. To make matters worse, I often mispronounce words or say idioms incorrectly. Embarrassing. People would make fun of or correct me. They still do, and it really gets under my skin.

Keeping my mouth shut was the best thing for me sometimes. When I opened it, what came out differed from what I intended to say. Feeling angry, can't focus, triggered and ready to explode. Thoughts were scrambled. This certainly didn't help others to understand who I was.

The day I set foot in my first Acadia university classroom was the start of a fresh change within me, and I did not know it was coming. I wanted to excel. If I wanted to do that, I had to get my shit together in the academic arena.

As a history major and minoring in sociology, I had to write many papers, take part in group discussions, and sometimes present my work in front of the class. This is where I learned to write and communicate better, things that I should have been able to learn in public school.

I discovered I loved to write and do research. Finally, I could share my opinions without being shot down. I strengthened my communication skills by learning to express my ideas and use evidence to support them. I was having intellectual conversations on paper, with my professors, and with my peers. It was exciting.

I committed 100%. I made the Dean's list, awarded many

scholarships and graduated among the top students in my B.A. and B.Ed. degrees.

But I still struggled inside. I had to work harder than the average student to overcome many communication obstacles while figuring out how to cope with all the emotions triggered by sounds.

Words didn't flow easily out of my mouth. If I had to speak up, my heart would pound so hard that I thought it would come out of my chest. I would tremble and sweat. My face would turn red. I just felt dumb, even though I wasn't.

Presentations were challenging. Everyone was watching me while I stood up in front of my classmates. The days leading up to it were a mess. During presentations, I was so emotional. A few times, I even became teary-eyed while presenting. Still, I wanted to do an outstanding job, so I pushed hard to control them. My classmates were incredibly supportive.

These struggles didn't just come from a sound trigger. This was how I always felt. It may have come from many years of feeling like this. Was this sound trauma? In junior and senior high, I would not do a presentation because when I tried, I couldn't do it. I froze in front of the classroom.

At Acadia, I finally was in a place where I wanted to push myself to be better. I wanted to learn and be above average. For the first time in my life, I felt smart. Others were seriously interested in my thoughts and ideas.

I developed relationships with my professors and always sat up front so I would hear every word they would say. Sometimes I would stay after class and talk with them or make an appointment to discuss ideas about a paper I wanted to write. I was a sponge, trying to soak up all the knowledge.

I felt accepted. I had never experienced anything like this in my life. Often, I asked, "How the hell did I get here, and how is it I am doing so well?" I could have become a lifelong university student. But that's what happens when you finally get the support you need to draw out of you the good stuff that is inside. I miss those days.

However, my new communication skills didn't transfer well outside of the university because when I took off my academic cap, I returned to my old self, but this time with a know-it-all attitude. Instead of remaining calm, I would get even hotter on discussing topics. "I know. I'm taking a course on that." I became an opinionated "right-fighter" and shot others down.

After discovering misophonia and telling others about it, conversations carried an authoritative tone even though I still didn't know much. My body language, facial expressions, word choices, the blame...no one wanted to listen to that and looking back, I don't blame them one bit. However, since I lived with it all my life, I felt like an expert and was angry about many things that happened to me.

Negative energy explosion. People wanted to avoid carrying the discussion on for long, and no wonder. I came across as overbearing and hostile whenever I spoke about misophonia.

I noticed how they reacted, and I took great offence to it. So, the conversations stopped. I went back to keeping quiet about my misophonia. Many years went by, sharing very little. Even as Facebook became increasingly popular, I didn't share on there.

It wasn't until I started writing this book that I opened up again. But this time, I'm using all the lessons I learned to tell my story more effectively so that people want to listen.

One of the best and most impactful communication lessons I learned from talking about my misophonia happened during my teaching practicum. It’s trickled into many other areas of my personal and business life when speaking to others about hard things. The experience opened up my eyes. I took so much from it and still use it today.

A requirement for my Bachelor of Education degree was to complete two teaching practicums for several weeks, one at a junior high level and the other at a senior high level. My first practicum was at a junior high level.

As a new teacher-in-training, I first introduced myself to my students by sharing a bit about my personal life. This helped to develop a better understanding and relatability between us.

Since I was spending much time in classrooms again, places filled with trigger sounds, I decided to discuss my misophonia. I did not expect what would happen.

My students tuned in. There were fascinated. I had their attention. They wanted to know more and were wowed that I was even talking about it. They asked many questions. They wanted to learn more.

Why the hell did this happen? How can it be that when talking to them, they reacted entirely differently than everyone else I spoke to about my misophonia?

I got to thinking about it for some time afterwards. The reason is this - I did it differently than I ever had done.

I gently spoke as I told my story, without blame or shame. I wanted my students to understand, more than anything, to see that I am a human and have struggles. I used a kind tone of voice filled with compassion. My body language and facial expressions were calm and relaxed, not tense and dramatic.

When I noticed I was capturing their full attention and that they were genuinely curious to learn more, I kept going with this new gentle flow. We even made some classroom rules together. They showed much respect, and they genuinely cared.

This was my first experience effectively communicating about my misophonia, except when I did my presentation in university, but that was different. That was an educational presentation. This was personal story-telling.

And I found it so easy to do with my students. I didn't get emotional. I kept it together. It was an incredible experience that set me on a new path for talking to others about my misophonia.

What does this new path look like?

First, using a softer and calmer tone of voice is vital. Second, being more aware of word choices is critical. I also relax my body language and face. That combo right there is more inviting to continue a discussion. It creates less tension and friction.

I invite and ask questions to establish a more profound understanding between us. A biggie is to talk more about how I feel inside and relate it to the actual sound instead of blaming the person making it. It has gone from a one-way discussion with me pointing fingers to a two-way one without finger-pointing.

People like that. I like this. I love it! I am developing a more effective way to explain my misophonia experiences and what I need to feel okay. We are now talking. Finally, I'm making headway.

I decided to try this approach with my teenage son and his friends. I made rules in the house, explained what the sounds did to me, and how important it was for my happiness.

They followed them. Sometimes we would make light jokes, but not in an offensive way. And if they made a sound, there was a quick apology. It took the edge off. Everyone showed respect. I felt like they cared.

Then I talked to my mom. We sat down. I told her I was sorry and that I didn't blame her. I know she carried much guilt in her heart for many years. I told her what I needed, and she was more than willing to help me. She would do whatever it would take.

The journey to repairing the damage from all those years could only begin with effective communication. Sure, it was challenging and took a very long time. However, it was necessary. And the journey isn't over.

About four years ago, my son said, "Mom. You should read this book. I think it would be really good for you."

"What book?"

"7 Habits of Highly Effective People by Stephen Covey. It's one of the best books I have ever read. You can borrow it."

I borrowed his book. I read it. It changed me.

I learned so much. And to be honest, I need to read it again. But one of the key takeaways was this "listen with the intention to understand, not the intent to reply" thing. I had never thought about it like that before.

I have been one that would formulate a response in my head while I so-called listened to the other person speak. And if I wasn't doing that, I was fighting some emotional battle from a sound trigger. I wasn't listening to anyone. No wonder I constantly faced a breakdown in communication. As I said before, it was a one-way street for me.

The first step was to start within me, train my brain to listen more and ask questions instead of telling them what I think right after, no matter how gentle my responses were becoming.

Because I often felt I could not express my thoughts or feelings for so long, I became eager to share what was on my mind. My ideas took priority.

This is rude, and it leaves others feeling like they are unheard. I felt like this much of my life, and I didn't like it, but here I was doing it to others.

When Tyler suggested that I read the book, I think he saw that in me and didn't want to say it out loud for fear of hurting my feelings. My boy is very soft-hearted and polite.

Reading the book made me realize I still had a ton to learn to communicate effectively. I wanted people to listen to understand me, and I needed to do the same for them.

It doesn't matter what I know about misophonia, how it impacts me, all my stories, etc. If I listen, I can communicate effectively. I must stop jumping in and taking over the conversations.

This is a life-long practice. Change takes time. There's always something to learn, to strengthen, to make better. It takes work. A lot of deep, challenging work. I had to be willing to accept that I was wrong, even when I had thought for so long that I was right.

Facing the reality that I was creating and deepening many of my problems and then stepping up to the plate to change that...I struggle even to find the words right now to explain how fucking hard that is on my soul, my heart, and my every being.

But accepting this hard truth allowed me to find myself and learn how to let my inner light shine.

And since I want to help create a better understanding and awareness about misophonia, it is necessary to talk about it to deliver the experiences I kept quiet about for so long.

The journey of living with misophonia keeps evolving. My mission is to talk about it so people can hear me, learn from me, and generate genuine compassion and support. And this book is a significant piece of that.

And so here I am, on my way.

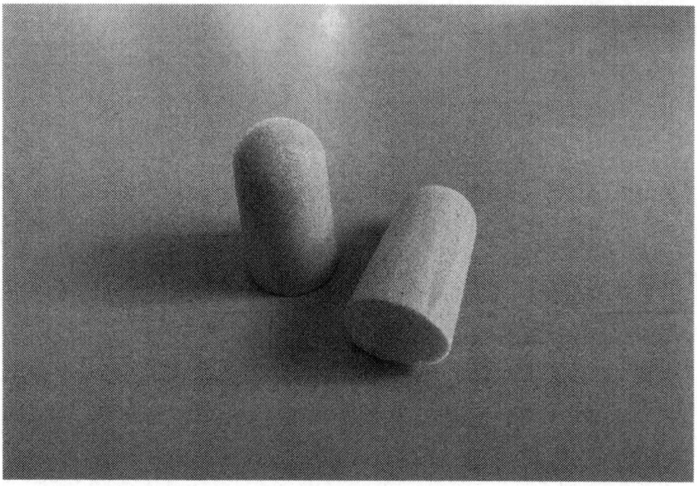

CHAPTER 12: COPING

Now, I want to dive into my story about how I learned to develop coping and communication strategies to calm down and create peace in my life.

Let's begin with my story of unknowingly coping.

Sometimes, I just hated everybody.
Sometimes, I just wanted to be deaf.

It's an awful thing wishing to be deaf. I dreamt about how it would bring me peace. I once tried to poke my eardrums with a knitting needle, another time with a pencil. I am glad I didn't.

But the question is this–did I develop coping mechanisms for a disorder that I didn't even know I had? Yes, I did. But how?

The obvious is plugging my ears with my fingers or cupping them with my hands. But I also found that sticking my earlobe in my ear while I watched TV or sat next to someone would help.

Then I started using earplugs when I was 18, but only for sleeping and at work in the fish plant where I was required to use them.

In school and public spaces, I would try to escape inside my mind by thinking about another place or focusing on something nearby, like the title on a book cover or a spot on the floor. That was hard and not effective, but it got me through.

Talking and moving about in public spaces helps. If I can spark a conversation or move around, I can at least mute or overpower some sounds.

At home, it was easy, as I would go to my room. Problem solved, except at the dinner table, which I suffered through. That was tough.

And then there was going outside, which was always a release. This became my great escape.

I never used anxiety pills or drugs to cope. However, I would be lying if I said I didn't have the odd glass of wine to take the edge off sometimes.

I noticed early in life that alcohol eased the tension. The more I drank, the less triggered I was, but that was part of another serious problem.

I had a love affair with alcohol for much of my life, and it almost destroyed me. A topic for another book...

So, this is pretty much it for coping with misophonia without even knowing I had the disorder. But honestly, I truly wasn't coping. I was releasing most of the rage and emotions by fighting with my family, beating on people, hitting things, hitting myself, drinking... that's not what I call coping.

As for daydreaming, fidgeting, escaping into nature, running to my room, and plugging my ears, you can call these coping. But it wasn't until I realized this disorder that I actively started investigating what others were doing, hearing their stories, and seeking ideas to develop more effective coping mechanisms intentionally.

And on that note, here are some ways I'm coping now. I've taken previous methods and made them better while exploring new ideas.

Coping #1 – Earplugs

Remember when I mentioned using my earlobe to help block out the sound? I would take my earlobe and tuck it in my earhole. I could even tilt my head until my ear touched my shoulder and then use my shoulder to tuck the earlobe up into my earhole and keep it there. Uncomfortable as hell!

And then I also mentioned how I started using earplugs when I was 18. It was those foam ones, and I still use them today.

I first started using them to help me sleep. But after I learned I had misophonia and discovered in Facebook groups how others were using them in public, I decided to try.

Wow, such a simple tool to help me out in times of desperate need. I feel embarrassed for not thinking of this sooner.

At first, I was scared people would see me using them. Now, I could care less what anyone thinks. My sanity is more important.

I have earplugs everywhere- throughout our home, my office, the truck, my jacket pockets, and several pairs in my purse. They are cheap, and Justin keeps me in good supply.

I remember one time he brought me home a big box of my favourite kind. The soft orange ones so that I can create a good seal. I can pull them out slightly or tuck them in deeper to control the sound levels.

People ask why I don't use music. I can't get the music to play fast in panic situations. It doesn't work as well as my cheap orange foam earplugs. The earplugs work more quickly. They are easy to shove in my ears, and I don't have to worry if whatever song is playing will trigger me too. Not all music is awesome for me.

In the past few years, I tried using Apple AirPods Pro. They claim they are noise cancelling, but they are not. They also make my ears sore. Earplugs are quickly accessible, and I can wear them everywhere, even during meetings. I want to try headphones, but I'll be limited in using them. Imagine putting them on in a meeting. Not gonna happen!

Some gadgets are now on the market, such as Loop and Calmer. I want to try them all, test them out and do reviews. I would be a great candidate, as my misophonia is at an extreme level with a growing list of severe triggers as I age. I have "sonic" hearing in my left ear. My mom always told me, "You hear things no one else can hear."

While earplugs don't completely block out the sounds, they can take the edge off, especially for high-pitched sounds. They can block them out for low sounds if I push them in my ears far enough.

Unfortunately, some sounds come with a vibration. Even without the sound, it still triggers me if I can feel the vibrations. Sometimes it's worse as I feel physically attacked by the sound. I will start swiping down my arms, rubbing my thighs with pressure, and feel my body prepare for a battle.

When I visit my parents now, the earplugs go in deep before I even enter the house. Now I can sit with them and talk without feeling frustrated by all the mouth and breathing sounds. I know there are too many triggers, so I prepare ahead. I wish I had these growing up.

Earplugs allow me to be with others in spaces that usually cause turmoil. While I still struggle with the visuals and vibrations, at least the noise is dissipated.

Some people have told me that if I overuse earplugs, it might strengthen the trigger, making me more sensitized as I don't learn to cope with the sound. I beg to differ, and the stories I shared in this book clearly say that it isn't a problem for me.

Earplugs make my life better, not worse. I suffered long enough. I'm not going to give up a natural, drug-free, inexpensive, and quickly accessible coping mechanism that helps me feel calmer and more in control when trigger sounds appear.

However, one area where earplugs do not work for me is talking on the telephone. The phone enhances mouth noises and can cause speech to sound distorted. But if I put in earplugs, I have difficulty hearing due to the different frequencies. If I turn down the volume, I miss out on words.

And I can't stand the speakerphone. It scratches my brain. I shake my head as I cringe my face and pace the floor. I mute people, and they don't even know it. I lose out on the conversation. I don't like to talk on the phone. Please send me an email instead.

Regardless, earplugs have become one of my main coping mechanisms and are inexpensive. They work most of the time, and I have other ways to cope when they don't.

Coping #2 – Escape Routes

If I want to find peace and keep it, I have to change things in my life. I don't want to be ruled by this disorder, but I can't help how I feel from it, so I have created "sound escapes".

If there is a place I want to go, such as the movies, where I might become trapped by sounds, I will tell the person I am with that if there are sound triggers and it gets bad, I will need to leave, and it's okay. This is my choice, and I do not expect anyone else to go with me.

Sometimes I am in a place where I don't know anyone, like a

grocery store or a bank, but I can leave if I need to, and I do. I don't feel bad about it. I go back another day. It's okay.

Now, with that said, I avoid being in high-trigger places as much as possible. Life is better if I avoid areas I know generally have more triggers. But this is only sometimes possible.

Sometimes I must be in certain places or be there to do an important task, such as taking a course or attending a medical appointment. In these situations, I rely mainly on my earplugs. I feel better if I can sit somewhere that distances me from others. If I can get up and walk around, that's the best.

I'm a curious person. I like exploring the world. But the older I get, the more places I avoid. For the sake of living a more peaceful life, it's a better choice to pick and choose depending on the day.

But there are all sorts of places I can still go. I have developed a fantastic connection with nature and find quiet places outside the most incredible areas to be for me. It is my happy place as long as it's free of barking dogs and many people. I can explore, feel free, and be at peace.

Someday, I hope to own a quiet little cottage on an oversized private lot in the woods on a lake, with no one living nearby. Not a sound, except what nature makes.

Coping #3 – Categorize People and Places

This is hard to admit. Based on their sounds, I place people, animals, and places under a trigger category. It is not just a way to cope, but a way to manage my life and the activities I want or need to do.

People, in general, produce the highest number of triggers. I find it more challenging to deal with when another human makes the noise than a thing or place with no feelings. I do not want to hurt other people's feelings. Sadly, I have done that far more often than I care to admit.

So, let's get this difficult part over with by first introducing the main categories.

Severe trigger
High trigger
Moderate trigger
Low to no trigger

Under each category, there is a list of triggers. The ones I listed at the beginning of this book will fall under these, mainly in the top two.

A high-trigger person will produce many noises that trigger me. They tend to be extremely difficult to be around, no matter how much I love them. Often, I have to limit my time with them or avoid them altogether. I can't even call them on the phone because it can hone in on every little sound they make, and it's right in my ear...which gets in my head, and I struggle to get rid of the sound long after the phone call is over.

As sad as this may sound, I have come to associate high-trigger people with their body size or age. Although this is not always the case, overweight and older people often make sounds that trigger me, such as breathing heavily, loud eating, grunting sounds from the movement they struggle to make, and a list of noises that come from their mouth or nose.

Also, when people are sick and sniffling, coughing, have difficulty breathing... I cannot stand this! God, I feel like a horrible, insensitive human right now.

People who make sounds that moderately trigger me can still make high-trigger sounds. They do it less often. I can be around them longer, depending on the day.

I can spend the entire day with low or no-trigger people and feel calm. But I don't have a lot of these people in my life. My misophonia is so extreme.

However, there is a trick I have learned. If I want to spend time with a high-trigger person, I can do so in a space with loud music (that I enjoy) or, better yet, be outside with the sounds of nature, such as on a hike. I try to avoid spaces where the noises high-trigger people make are amplified, such as visiting someone at home or calling them on the phone.

And suppose it's a stranger or someone new I meet. In that case, it usually only takes one visit to know which category they fall under because the thing is this - I may forget their name, but I won't forget the noises they make. It embedded the memory in my brain that even when I see them next, it's how I immediately identify them in my head.

"Oh, she is the tongue-smacking person," or "he is the extremely heavy breather when he is eating."

It's the sad truth, but it's the way I am. It will never change. This is how I cope, trying to escape the sound traps constantly.

I have a growing database of trigger sounds in my brain, where I tag and organize people, animals, things, and places by their trigger sounds. Depending on the type and number of tags they have, I will then place them on the severe, high, moderate, or low to no trigger list.

It is challenging to understand, but I know this system I developed. I use it to guide me, as I do not want to be subjected to the sounds and emotional upheaval.

This is not about the people. It's not about who they are. This is about me.

And I refuse to go around and tell everyone what category they fall in and say things that will tear them down to improve my life. I am not about to tell everyone to stop making sounds, either. I am the one that has to figure this out.

But I want people to understand that I have to protect my

emotional well-being, and part of that is dealing with this disorder in the way it will help me.

Coping #4: Mimicking the Sound

'Ugh. He's eating chips. Okay, where are the chips?'

You know the saying, "If you can't beat 'em, might as well join 'em."

Mimicking someone else's sound helps me release the pressure and tension. This is both an impulse and a deliberate reaction.

I sometimes mimic people without deliberate intention. It's a compulsive reaction when it gets to the boiling point. It's weird when it happens. For example, someone is flicking their tongue, and while I'm going insane in my brain, the next thing I notice, I am doing it too.

If it's a stranger, I stop. But if it was someone I knew and I was out of control, I'll get up in their face and continue exaggerating the noise, showing them what they were doing to me and how the sound made me crazy. Awkward.

Though, I don't behave like this anymore. It was a rude way for me to react, and it had to stop. And it didn't help me in any way. It made me look like I was crazy.

But I mimic people deliberately, in a non-invasive way to cope and help me get through the moment.

An intentional mimic is eating chips when another person eats chips. If she types on a keyboard, I must type on the keyboard. If he clicks his pen, I must click my pen. And so on...

It's easier to cope this way when you know someone. I can do what they are doing, and it doesn't seem awkward. But imagine trying to mimic a stranger, such as a shopper in your aisle browsing the same product as you, and they start whistling a tune, and so do you. It would create a strange moment.

It's a struggle. I want so badly to mimic the sound that

someone else is making. Or I need to get away from that person immediately.

But why am I so compelled to mimic the sound when I'm next to someone? Because it gives me a sense of control which can help calm me down. For example, I will eat the chips for as long as he eats his chips, and everything will be okay.

When it gets to the boiling point where I'm losing control and mimicking the sound angrily and disgustingly, it feels more like I now have to fight and try to shut that sound down.

When possible, I will go to another room and mimic the sound until I get out of my head. Sometimes, even when the sound stops, I can still hear it. I need to release it. I have done this at home, in bathrooms, restaurants, and wherever I can find a private space to let go.

When I make the sound in private, it is done in a wildly exaggerated way. It's not how the person was. It's my magnified version so I can get the fucking noise out of my head.

I can't tell you how often I wanted to stand on my back deck and start barking along with all the other dogs in my neighbourhood. I envision how good it would feel to release it, how good it would feel to let that anger out, and how crazy I would look to the rest of the world.

Imagine a 50-year-old woman standing on her deck barking like a mad person, more aggressively and louder than all the other dogs. If I could get away with doing this, I would do it. Maybe...probably not. But I certainly think about doing it and how good it would feel.

Mimicking is a coping mechanism, but it's not one I prefer to do. It's effective sometimes, as in chip-eating situations. However, most of the time, I look away, put my earplugs in, and go somewhere else in my mind. I seek to escape.

You see why misophonia is so hard to explain and understand. There's just so much to unpack. And everyone with misophonia learns to cope differently. You must find what works for you, but you must also be deliberate and mindful. It can get exhausting. It takes time. It takes years.

So, to sum things up, my primary coping mechanisms are:

- earplugs
- escape routes
- categorizing
- physical distancing
- deliberately mimicking the sound

Living a life with misophonia is a hard road to travel. Finding ways to cope is hard. But it's necessary if I ever want to feel more peaceful as I move forward.

I've been angry for far too long.

Now the journey is about finding my peace and calm.

CHAPTER 13: MY GREAT ESCAPE

The journey to finding my peace and calm? Let's now dive into that. It changed how I cope with misophonia and every facet of my life. I call it My Great Escape.

It isn't a coping mechanism that I practice when triggered. It is more of a way to release the build-up of stored tension from the triggers. I am improving my overall well-being and helping me heal from the past.

First, movement! Any movement relieves me, but the most incredible escape is doing it outside in nature. I can feel the pressure dissipating from my body and mind as I travel through a trail, swim in the ocean, run through a field, and dance under the stars. I'll take any movement I can get. The more I can do it and how I want, the better it feels.

It adds to the pain and suffering if I am forced to sit still. I have been offered pills to help calm me down. That is not how this woman rolls. I'm not knocking anyone who does. I'm talking about myself. Movement outside is MY pill.

Here's how it developed...

I grew up in a tiny fishing community, and we lived on a quiet dirt road. Our neighbourhood was safe. We knew all our neighbours and family lived nearby. I had the beach and woods to play in. It was the perfect playground for a child, all along a 1-km strip of God's country.

I wasn't involved in school sports, as they were filled with negative experiences. Not only did I have to deal with the sounds of bouncing balls, squeaky sneakers, kids screaming, and that god-awful whistle echoing inside the gym walls, but I was also often bullied and picked on by other kids. To top it off, my gym teachers didn't see any athletic potential in me, which was clearly stated in how they treated me.

Anyway, my "gym" is, and always has been, the great outdoors. Mom and Dad didn't have to tell me twice to "go outside." It was where I always wanted to go, even to play or sit in the yard. I enjoyed all the seasons and found something new to explore in each one. Being outside gave me freedom, where I could just be myself.

Growing up was all about play, riding bikes, swimming, climbing trees, pond skating, sledding, playing in old cars back in the woods, wandering around the neighbourhood, and going on little neighbourhood adventures.

I did my fitness outside under the open sky with the smell of the grass, the wind blowing through my hair, and trees telling me their stories...all of nature's energy. I soaked it up. It became a part of me.

I remember taking long walks through the woods as a kid. I wanted to see where the paths would go and get lost in the woods, not literally, just figuratively. To this day, I'm still curious when I see a new trail. I want to follow it and see where it will lead me, thinking, "What will I discover today?"

The sounds in nature are calming. Nothing triggers me, not even birds chirping. I love the wind through the trees, sitting by a babbling brook or listening to the waves crashing on the beach shore. These sounds are nature's music. Listening to it lifts me up and fills my soul with positivity.

At around 18 years old, I became more interested in running and weightlifting. Little did I know then that I would eventually complete an iron-distance triathlon (3.8k swim + 180k bike + 42.2k run), own a fitness company, and become a canfitpro PRO Trainer to help others become certified in the fitness industry.

I sought more ways to occupy myself and create actual excuses to move. I borrowed a book from my brother, 'The New Encyclopedia of Modern Bodybuilding' by Arnold Schwarzenegger. After reading it from cover to cover, I set up a home gym and began experimenting with weightlifting.

And this journey continued, but on another level. The more I explored weightlifting, the more I craved the release and relief it gave me.

Lifting was something I fell in love with. I pumped iron 6 x per week, doing splits and double splits. Even though I never intended to compete, I trained like a competitor. I kept quiet about what I was doing. Social media didn't exist back then.

I lifted at home and logged every rep, set, and pound. I was hooked. Thirty years later, I still have those log sheets. And yes, I am still lifting weights.

In 1999, I pursued the YMCA Individual Conditioning course.

Then in 2000, I became a canfitpro Personal Trainer Specialist. My first gig was volunteering at our local YMCA as a personal trainer.

In 2001, I attended my first group fitness class at a local boutique fitness studio. The class instructor was also the business owner. After class, she approached me.

"If you get certified as a fitness instructor, I'll give you a job."

I couldn't believe what I was hearing. The owner saw something in me that no one else ever did.

So, I signed up for the canfitpro Fitness Instructor Specialist certification course, completed it, and she hired me, as she said she would. This kind and beautiful soul was not just my boss. She became my mentor. And this entire experience transformed my life.

This was the first time I felt supported and encouraged in physical fitness because someone saw something special in me. I blossomed, and my mentor encouraged the blooming. Not only did she help me grow, but so did her members. I remain connected to many of them today.

Personal training is exciting, but it can be challenging because of working closely with people and discovering the sounds they make. Sometimes working one-on-one with people would trap me with a person who triggered me.

I didn't find that in group fitness and had very few experiences where I was trigged in a group fitness setting. There is a more significant energy release through teaching a group too. The music is loud, we are all moving, it's busy, it's fun, and it was a positive outlet that I found highly stimulating. It is much more dynamic, and I get to participate. Plus, I could keep a distance.

I remember the first time I taught a group fitness class. I was so scared. My mentor boosted me up, and the members were very accepting and supportive. Everything unfolded nicely. I found my place, my jam, and my people.

I was allowed to play. Wait, I wasn't just allowed to play. I was asked to be the leader. I built confidence and self-esteem and finally felt like I fit in somewhere.

I never got asked to be a leader in school. I was never a captain of a sports team. I always felt left out, was picked last, and the teachers never saw anything in me.

I continued to teach at this gym for a few more years until I decided to attend university to become a school teacher. I had to say goodbye. It was a sad moment. They threw me a farewell party. I will never forget it.

I went back to lifting in my home gym and running my local roads to stay connected with movement and provide me with the positive outlet I needed.

At this point, I was also working as a manager at a local Inuit art gallery. One day, a woman came into the gallery and handed me a pamphlet about the Bridgewater Triathlon Club. I didn't even know it existed.

She was incredibly excited, happy, and full of energy. Looking at her, as awful as this sounds, I would have never guessed she was a triathlete. What does a triathlete look like? I didn't even know, but I know now that it looks like anyone because looks have nothing to do with it.

Anyway, I thought, "if she can do it, so can I." After asking my friend to join me, we went to the first meetup. I was hooked and spent the next eight years in this club.

For the second time in my life, I found a place where I fit. I could swim, bike, and run and do it all outside. While I loved teaching fitness classes, I loved these outdoor sports more. Now I'm in nature, and I was hooked.

The club members were kind, encouraging, and motivating. They showed genuine care and concern. I felt they believed in me, even though I was a total newbie. I used a mountain bike with slicks, cotton clothes, and cheap running shoes. I had no swim cap or goggles. I didn't have fancy gadgets or gear or any knowledge about triathlons either. None of that seemed to matter.

Joining the tri club changed my life's direction and meant everything to me. I had bigger goals. I was learning a new skill and going to the races. I made new friends that were not into drugs and alcohol. I was doing stuff I never thought I would ever do. It was a full-on commitment. The tri club became family.

I found my place. I had something to focus on that also served as a positive outlet for anger, rage, depression, and confusion. Swimming, biking, running... I was transforming my anger into calm.

I was exactly where I needed to be. Finally, I could prove to others that I am not weak. I am competent, and I am committed to trying my best, and I will work hard. I am an athlete!

Joining the triathlon club was a gateway to realizing that sports were the answer I needed all my life. I often wondered how things would have turned out had I been given more opportunities in school.

I could channel my negative energy into positive energy, which I needed. Here is where I could get my head screwed on straight, think, solve life problems, and take as much time as necessary to work through them while I swam, biked and ran.

When I discovered I had misophonia and started reading more articles about it, I began to understand better why exercise and movement gave me a natural way to cope and calm down. It was my pill.

I became an endurance athlete. After eight years of doing triathlons, I moved to cycling and snowboarding. I have also competed in road races, cyclocross, and mountain biking.

Even more so than triathlon, mountain biking is my authentic jam. I'm riding through the woods, just givn'r, letting it all out. Well, there's no better feeling except being on a snowboard, which is the next closest thing.

There's much more to tell about how sports, fitness and wellness evolved and changed my life. I could write a book about it. But I've said enough for you to understand better how that connection developed and what it's done for my life in every aspect, with misophonia, with my anger, confidence, and overall well-being...

I had formed such a strong bond with all these outdoor fitness sports that I eventually became an NCCP Adult Community Triathlon Coach, a level one CASI Snowboard Instructor, a level one PMBIA Mountain Bike Instructor, and also a TrainingPeaks level 1 accredited coach. It made so much sense to do so because in helping others, I am also helping myself.

These sports saved my life. They were the answer. I can't imagine a life without them. I wanted others to feel the positive change that can happen in one's life through sport.

It's not about being the best. It's not about making the podium, although it's pretty cool when it happens. But it is about finding yourself, finding freedom, building confidence and empowering yourself to take control of your potential at every level.

Fitness is the answer. It's always been the answer. It continues to be the answer. Just look up the numerous studies out there. Listen to real experts such as Dr. Stuart Phillips, Dr. Brad Schoenfeld, and others in their respective fields.

We know that fitness can help us - physically, mentally, and emotionally. That spills over into every other area of one's life.

It's an outlet—a positive one. And Lord knows, in living with misophonia, I needed a positive outlet. The best part about this is that it can look however you want it to look. There are no set rules.

You can create your own.

I now teach people how to do this, find what makes their heart beat happy, and help them make their flow work for them, so they reap the benefits and keep reaping them for years to come.

And now you understand better why this topic had to have a chapter of its own. Time with nature, all types of movement, exercise, sports... holistic well-being and lifestyle. I developed this to save myself, heal, cope, and escape.

I will never let go. I will continue to live like this until I die.

CHAPTER 14: FINDING MY MOM

All those years, I hated her. All those years, I loved her.

I chose to lose her. I wanted to be around her, but yet I didn't. I couldn't. So many tears and years of struggles to try and love each other.

But when we finally met, and we both understood what was going on, that's when I started to find my Mom.

Now, I can sit with her and talk for hours. I ask her questions about her life. I often ask her for the recipes she tried to teach me as a child. Now I go to her when I need advice for everything she was never allowed to tell me in my younger years as I pushed her out of my world.

"Mom, can you teach me how to make homemade bread?"

I was 46, and she was 67. Her heart was glowing. I could see it shining on her face. She could teach me how to make homemade bread because I finally let her in.

I can hug her now, for a long time. I can sit next to her on the couch and lie on her shoulder. I can visit her without having to leave right away.

And believe it or not, Mom is one of the few people I can talk to on the phone for hours because we make it work, and we can do so with love and compassion.

I can be with her. I never had that. I took it from me. It hurts because it didn't have to be that way. For so much of my life, I battled her. I blamed her for everything wrong with me. I had decided that she was the problem.

But she wasn't the problem. Misophonia and my behaviour was the problem.

Even though we spent so much time at war, when I decided to try to find her, she was already there waiting for me, with so much love, compassion, and forgiveness.

I discovered my mom is a pretty special person. I don't know any other woman like her. She hasn't had an easy life yet she is the strongest woman I know. Mom is full of empathy, acceptance, and forgiveness. She thrives on helping others. It makes her feel good.

She was like this all along. I didn't know. I always saw her attempt to help me as trying to control me. I could never tell her what was going on inside me. Things could have been so different.

Over the past ten years, Mom and I have made considerable strides in our relationship. We can't even imagine hurting each other now. It would pain us too much. We know what we have, and it is precious to our lives. This is what we need. Nothing stops us now that we have it.

I still have much healing to do regarding my relationship with my mom. Writing this book has helped me dig deeper into my past and come face to face with things I was still pushing down. It's worse than I thought it was. It took great strength and many tears to own up to my past and how I treated her. She was easy to blame for my issues.

I find this challenging to write about because I'm still searching inside me, trying to figure things out from my past.

However, I am also smiling because of what we have built over the past several years since we joined our hearts together. We never wasted another moment. Time with each other has become more precious than ever.

Finally, I found my mom, even though she was right there before me for all those years. With our hearts now joined, we could help each other become whole again.

And we finally have what we both wanted all those years.

I love you, Mom.
I feel so very blessed that you're mine.
Thank you for never giving up on me.

CHAPTER 15: IF ONLY WE HAD KNOWN

I wish there were such a thing as time travel. I lost so much because of this disorder, and most of it was during a time when no one even knew about it. But now we do know. And better than ever. So, we continue to move forward in learning better ways to live with misophonia.

But, if I could go back in time, and we could know about it, here are some things I wish I would have had to help me live a better life. Some of these things can shed light on what you can do for yourself or someone living with misophonia.

No labels. The labels still live in me today. I realize my parents didn't understand, and I'm not placing blame. Being called a hateful snip was hard to shake. Was I hateful? Yes. Do I forgive my parents? Absolutely. That's part of my healing.

Therapy. My teenage behaviour wasn't acceptable or normal. I felt like I had nobody. I needed professional help. When I finally reached out at age 22, it was one of the best things I ever did for myself.

A quiet place to learn. At home, I could do my homework in my room, but I had no place to go at school. I wish I had had a soundproof room, especially when I needed to focus on projects and tests. I wish I had this throughout all my school years, including Acadia university. Focus rooms are a thing now. I've seen them online, and they look dreamy. I'd love to try one.

Freedom to escape. When things start to run hot, the best way for me to cool down is to get away from the sounds and anything else that goes along with it, such as feeling ashamed, trapped, and panicked. Many times, I had to try and survive through it. I have sound memories, and they still trigger my emotions. It would have made a big difference in my life if I had escaped the sound that triggered me. I genuinely believe the more extended periods have contributed to PTSD.

A positive outlet. I needed something physical - movement. To be able to release tension and transform negative energy into positive energy would have been an excellent way for me to flush out pent-up anger. I wish I had been encouraged in school to join sports, supported by my teachers, and accepted by my peers. The complete opposite happened. Knowing what sports and fitness have done for me as an adult could have helped me with my behavioural and self-esteem problems as a child.

Genuine compassion and support. In any relationship, when you feel misunderstood and have assumptions made about you, it can beat you down. Things changed when I started to feel heard, believed, and genuinely supported. I wish people would have talked with me more and asked about my feelings. I just wanted to feel like I was loved and accepted by others. But I didn't, so I was constantly battling that on top of misophonia.

Accommodations in the workplace. Work environments, school systems, and any type of organization where people have to come together for a common purpose should have accommodations for people with misophonia. I can't do my best work if I'm fighting a battle inside my head whenever a sound is made that triggers me.

I feel frustrated when I try to explain what is happening, and co-workers shrug it off because they do not believe it to be real. At the same time, I can't expect everyone to tiptoe around me. That doesn't create a productive working environment either.

I wanted to be a school teacher, but unfortunately, it didn't work out. I eventually learned I needed to choose careers more suitable for my misophonia. That's a big reason I have been a boss for most of my work life. I currently own my second company and am celebrating ten years in business.

Complete 100% noise-cancelling headphones. If I had had these in my younger years and been allowed to wear them when I needed to, things definitely would have been better for me. But they still have limitations, such as wearing them in meetings and lectures. However, someday I'm going to own a pair. I will wear them on the airplane, guaranteed.

I hope the ideas above help. Back in my younger days, we didn't know that misophonia existed. Now that we do, we can do better to help those living with it.

CLOSING MESSAGE

Even though I knowingly have had misophonia for 13 years, I am only now truly beginning to speak up about it and how it has impacted my life. This book has fueled the desire to continue the conversation and help others.

Misophonia is challenging to discuss, especially when you often feel shut down whenever you talk about it. There is still so much to learn about the disorder, but so much is also now known since it's discovery. However, there needs to be more awareness, and I hope this book ignites discussions and gives a voice to those who suffer in silence.

I want to support anyone with misophonia who feels alone, misunderstood, and struggling to find their way. I hope that within these pages you found a safe place, compassion and empathy. You can trust that you have someone who truly [illegible]rstands what you're dealing with daily and can help you feel [illegible] I got you.

How to connect with me?

Email: tammy@gofitlife.ca
Website: https://gofitlife.ca
Facebook: @trappedinsound & @gofitlifecoach
Instagram: @trappedinsound

How would I like to create more awareness?

I would be open to discussing the following:

- presentations in schools and organizations.
- be a guest on podcasts, vodcasts, or interviews
- translating this book into other languages

Also, if you are curious about my fitness and wellness online coaching services and programs, feel free to reach out. Email me at the address provided. We can have a little chit-chat about how your personal goals and go from there.

Of course, if you just want to send me your thoughts or feedback about my book, I invite you to email me too. I will read it, and yes, I will respond.

Once again, thank you so much for your support. Please help me to create more awareness by telling others about this book.

In peace and happiness,

Tammy Lee

AFTERWORD

Thank you so much for reading my book. Did you read between the lines? My story... it's not just about living with misophonia. It's more than that. It is about...

Love, anger, trust, disrespect. Being real.

Feeling misunderstood, but finding strength and courage to push through and keep reaching.

Standing up for yourself, even when you are standing alone.

Not letting your life to be stolen from you.

Going to battle with your demons to find peace within.

Being kind to yourself to learn how to be kinder to others.

The powerful impact of a mother-daughter relationship.

And most important of all, it's about forgiveness.

Whether you have misophonia or not, I hope my story made a positive impact on your life.

ACKNOWLEDGEMENT

Special thanks to my proofreaders for their helpful contributions: Nancy Slauenwhite (my mom), Helena Trenholm, Mike Dorsey, and Doreen Matthews

Photography credits: all photos except for two were either taken by me, my parents or a close friend.

Photo credit for chapter 1: Debbie Willis.

Photo credit for chapter 13: John Gibson Photo. John took this photo of me during the TransRockies Classic 7-day mountain bike stage race in 2019.

Book cover: the photo on the front is a picture of me in a position that I have found myself in a thousand times. The cover design represents the loneliness I often felt throughout my life. The graphics on my skin represent the emotions of rage, anger, and hate I feel throughout my body when triggered. The cover has a deeper meaning. It's hard to explain it all in a few words but if you read my story, you probably understand.

CITATION AND RESOURCES

Cited Source:

(1) Tinnitus and Hyperacusis Clinic. 'Misophonia Overview.' https://www.tinnitusclinicminnesota.com/misophonia-overview/ Accessed November 7, 2022.

Additional Resources:

Misophonia Institute
https://misophoniainstitute.org/what-is-misophonia/

soQuiet
https://www.soquiet.org/

Misophonia Association
https://misophonia-association.org/

Misophonia Podcast
https://www.misophoniapodcast.com/

ABOUT THE AUTHOR

Tammy Lee Slauenwhite

Tammy Lee was born in 1972 and grew up in Riverport, Nova Scotia, a tiny fishing village. She is a proud mom, teacher, fitness and wellness lifestyle coach, and endurance athlete. This is her first book, and she is planning to write another. When she's not teaching or writing, you can find her outside playing bikes, snowboarding or exploring a new trail. Visit her online at www.gofitlife.ca or on Facebook @gofitlifecoach. You can also email her at tammy@gofitlife.ca

Printed in Great Britain
by Amazon

22057892R00075